A Handy Classical and Mythological Dictionary for Popular Use

Harry Charles Faulkner

This work has been selected by scholars as being culturally important, and is part of the knowledge base of civilization as we know it. This work was reproduced from the original artifact, and remains as true to the original work as possible. Therefore, you will see the original copyright references, library stamps (as most of these works have been housed in our most important libraries around the world), and other notations in the work.

This work is in the public domain in the United States of America, and possibly other nations. Within the United States, you may freely copy and distribute this work, as no entity (individual or corporate) has a copyright on the body of the work.

As a reproduction of a historical artifact, this work may contain missing or blurred pages, poor pictures, errant marks, etc. Scholars believe, and we concur, that this work is important enough to be preserved, reproduced, and made generally available to the public. We appreciate your support of the preservation process, and thank you for being an important part of keeping this knowledge alive and relevant.

A HANDY
CLASSICAL AND MYTHOLOGICAL
DICTIONARY

FOR POPULAR USE.

WITH SEVENTY ILLUSTRATIONS.

A BRIEF AND CONCISE EXPLANATION OF THE ANCIENT MYTHOLOGICAL, BIOGRAPHICAL, HISTORICAL AND GEOGRAPHICAL ALLUSIONS MOST FREQUENTLY MET WITH IN ENGLISH LITERATURE.

BY H. C. PAULKNER,

Author of "A Handy Dictionary of Synonyms."

NEW YORK:

A. L. BURT, PUBLISHER.

PREFACE.

THE LITERATURE and Art of Greece and Rome has not only furnished the models from which all that is best in subsequent literature and art has been formed, but English Literature, both of the past and the present, as well as the literature of all other civilized nations, is overflowing with allusions to the writings of ancient Greek and Latin authors. The great English historians, poets, philosophers, essayists and novelists make constant reference to the Mythology, History, Biography and Geography of the ancients. In Art, representations of classical deities and heroes confront us in every gallery and museum, and modern artists and sculptors find a never-failing treasury of subjects in the myths and legends of the past. Even the newspapers, in the course of their discussion of the topics of the day, make continual use of classical allusions to aid in pointing the useful moral, or adorning the entertaining tale. In ordinary speech, countless classical references and comparisons have become proverbial.

It is the intention of this little volume to provide the ordinary reader with brief and concise explanations of the more important of these references, those which are absolutely necessary to a complete comprehension of much that otherwise loses half its force, if, indeed, it be not wholly unintelligible.

A popular Handbook of this kind has long been needed. There are great Classical Dictionaries, for the use of scholars and students, admirably complete, and covering the vast ground with a thoroughness that leaves nothing to be desired; but such books contain a great deal, both of fact and discussion, that is of value only to the scholar, and by reason of their very completeness, their diffusiveness, their size and their technicality, are not adapted for the average reader. The present volume is unlike any other existing work in another respect, it includes all the departments of classical allusions, mythological, biographical, historical and geographical. There have been Classical Dictionaries, Mythological Dictionaries and Ancient Atlases, but until now these divisions have never been collected into one comprehensive whole.

Additional value is obtained by the introduction of Egyptian,

Scandinavian and Hindoo Mythology, references to which constantly occur in our literature.

Notwithstanding necessary condensation, a proper balance has been maintained throughout; the more important topics have been treated at as great a length as the limited space would allow and less important ones have been disposed of more briefly. As it is of importance to discriminate between the Greek and Roman Mythology; the separate designations are given in each case—for example: Zeus (Jupiter). Careful attention has been paid to indicating the proper pronunciation; the illustrative quotations from the poets have been specially selected with the intention of assisting the reader in determining the proper syllabication and pronunciation. Particular care has been taken in the mythological allusions to avoid all indelicacy. A large number of illustrations have been introduced to exhibit the use that has been made of Mythology in both ancient and modern art.

In compiling this volume frequent use has been made of Dr. Smith's exhaustive "Classical Dictionary," (Anthon), the same author's dictionaries of "Greek and Roman Biography and Mythology," the famous but somewhat obselete work of Lempriere, Rowdens' "Pagan Deities," the excellent works of Gruber, Mannert, and Forbiger, two excellent English works by an anonymous author "A Handy Classical Dictionary" and "A Handbook of Mythology" (London, 1878), and many other volumes of less authority.

The chief difficulty in the making of this volume arose from the vastness of the subject and the copiousness of the materials. A Handbook for popular use must be convenient, clear, concise, and correct. It must never be technical, never fragmentary. Abreviation is necessary, but merely an abreviation of expression, not of fact. Nothing must be included that is unimportant, nothing omitted that is important. Fullness, and at the same time brevity, must be its essential characteristics.

How far this work is successful in furnishing a skeleton key to hitherto closed chambers of knowledge, is for the reader to decide. The compiler in submitting this HANDY CLASSICAL AND MYTHOLOGICAL DICTIONARY to the Public, can only point out what he considers its four claims to the consideration of an intelligent audience, viz.—

1st. Its COMPREHENSIVENESS. It contains a variety of topics never before included in one volume.

2nd. Its CONCISENESS. It presents this mass of matter in a handy pocket volume.

3rd. Its CLEARNESS. It is written in popular language, absolutely free from bewildering technicalities.

4th. Its CORRECTNESS, which has been assured by the greatest care in the comparison of authorities.

H. C. F.

NEW YORK, 1884.

A Handy Classical and Mythological Dictionary.

A

A'BAS, a son of Meganira, was turned into a water-lizard, for profaning the ceremonies of the Sacrifice.

ABDE'RUS. A friend of Hercules, after whom the town Abderus is named.

ABSYR'TUS, brother of Medea, and killed by her.

ABY'DOS. 1. A city of Asia opposite Sestos in Europe. It is famous as the scene of the love of Hero and Leander, and for the bridge of boats which Xerxes built there across the Hellespont. Leander was in the habit of swimming across the Hellespont to see Hero, till at length, on a stormy night, he was drowned. 2. A town in Egypt, where was a famous temple of Osiris.

ACADE'MI'A. A garden near Athens, originally belonging to Academus, from whom the name is derived. Here Plato opened his school of philosophy, and from this every place sacred to learning has ever since been called Academia.

ACADE'MUS. An Attic hero who betrayed Helen to Castor and Pollux. For this the Lacedemonians were always grateful, and whenever they invaded Attica always left his ground untouched.

ACHA'IA. A district in the northeastern part of the Greek peninsula.

ACHA'TES. A friend of Æneas whose fidelity was so exemplary that *Fidus Achates* has become a proverbial expression for a faithful friend.

ACHELO'US. The son of Oceanus and Terra, or Tethys, god of the river of the same name in Epirus. As one of the numerous suitors of Dejanira, he entered the lists against Hercules, and being inferior, changed himself into a serpent, and afterwards into an ox. Hercules broke off one of his horns and defeated him, after which, according to some, he was changed into a river, which has since been called Achelous.

ACH'ERON. One of the rivers of the infernal regions to which the shades of the dead resorted, and waited there till Charon, the ferryman, took them over.

> "Infernal rivers that disgorge
> Into the burning lake their baleful streams.
> . . . Sad Acheron, of sorrow black and deep."
> MILTON.

ACHIL'LES, the son of Peleus and Thetis, was the bravest of all the Greeks in the Trojan war. During his infancy Thetis plunged him in the Styx, thus making every part of his body invulnerable except the heel by which she held him. To prevent him from going to the Trojan war, Thetis sent him privately to the court of Lycomedes, where he was disguised in a female dress. As Troy could not be taken without his aid, Ulysses went to the court of Lycomedes in the habit of a merchant, and exposed jewels and arms for sale. Achilles, chosing the arms, discovered his sex, and went to the war. Vulcan made him a strong suit of armor, which was proof against all weapons. He was deprived by Agamemnon of his favorite Briseis, and for this affront he would not appear on the field till the death of Patroclus impelled him to vengeance. He slew Hector, who had killed Patroclus, and tying his corpse to his war-car, dragged it three times round Troy. He is said to have been killed by Paris, who inflicted a mortal wound in his vulnerable heel with an arrow. He is the great hero of Homer's Iliad.

ACIDA'LIA, a surname of Venus derived from a well in Bœotia.

A'CIS. A shepherd of Sicily, son of Faunus and the nymph Simæthis. Galatea passionately loved him, upon which his rival, Polyphemus, crushed him to death with a piece of broken rock. The gods changed Acis into a stream, which rises from Mount Ætna (Ovid).

ACROCERAUN'IA. A promontory of Epirus. Very dangerous to vessels.

ACTÆ'ON. A famous huntsman, son of Aristæus and Antonoe, daughter of Cadmus. He saw Diana (Artemis) and her attendants bathing, for which he was changed into a stag and devoured by dogs.

AC'TIUM. A town and promontory of Epirus, famous for the naval victory which Augustus obtained over Antony and Cleopatra, B. C. 31.

A'DES or HADES. The god of hell among the Greeks; the same as the Pluto of the Latins. The word is often used for hell itself by the ancient poets.

ADHER'BAL. Son of Micipsa, and grandson of Masinissa, was put to death by his brother Jugurtha, after vainly imploring the aid of Rome, B. C. 112.

ADME'TUS. Son of Pheres and Clymene, king of Pheræ in Thessaly, husband of Alcestis. Apollo, when banished from heaven, is said to have tended his flocks for nine years.

ADO'NIS, son of Cinyras and Myrrha, was the favorite of Venus. He was fond of hunting, and was often cautioned not to hunt wild beasts. This advice he slighted, and at last was mortally wounded by a wild boar. Venus changed him into the flower anemone. Proserpina is said to have restored him to life, on condition that he should spend six months of the year with her, and the rest of the year with Venus. This implies the alternate return of summer and winter. Shakespare, in "Venus and Adonis," thus alludes to the changing of Adonis into a flower:—

"By this the boy that by her side lay kill'd
Was melted like a vupor from her sight,
And in his blodd, that on the ground lay spill'd,
A purple flower sprung up, checkered with white,
Resembling well his pale cheeks, and the blood
Which in round drops upon their whiteness stood."

ADRAS'TUS, son of Talaus and Lysimache, was king of Argos. Polynices, being banished from Thebes by his brother Eteocles, fled to Argos, where he married Argia, daughter of Adrastus. The king assisted his son-in-law, and marched against Thebes with an army. He was defeated with great slaughter, and fled to Athens, where Theseus gave him assistance, and was victorious. Adrastus died from grief occasioned by the death of his son Ægialeus.

ADRIA'NUS, or HAD'RIAN. A famous emperor of Rome. He is represented as an active, learned, warlike, and austere general. He went to Britain, where he built a wall between the modern towns of Carlisle and Newcastle-on-Tyne, to protect the Britons from the incursions of the Caledonians.

ADSCRIPTI'TII DII were the gods of the second grade.

Æ'ACIDES. A name given to the descendents of Aracus, among them Peleus, Achilles and Pyrrhus. Aracus was a son of Jupiter, and after death became one of the judges of the lower regions.

ÆCAS'TOR, an oath used only by women, referring to the Temple of Castor.

ÆD'EPOL, an oath used by both men and women, referring to the Temple of Pollux.

ÆDI'LES. Roman magistrates, who had charge of all buildings, baths, and aqueducts, and examined weights and measures. The office of an Ædile was honorable, and the primary step to a more distinguished position in the State.

ÆGE'ON, a giant with fifty heads and one hundred arms, who was imprisoned by Jupiter under Mount Ætna. He must be regarded as the personification of earthquakes, etc.

Æ'GEUS. King of Athens, son of Pandion. Being desirous of having children, he went to consult the oracle, and on his return stopped at the court of Pittheus, king of Trœzene, who gave him his daughter Æthra in marriage. He directed her, if she had a son, to send him to Athens as soon as he could lift a stone under which he had concealed his sword. Æthra became mother of Theseus, whom she sent to Athens with his father's sword, Ægeus being at that time living with Medea, the divorced wife of Jason. When Theseus came to Athens, Medea attempted to poison him, but he escaped; and upon showing Ægeus the sword, discovered himself to be his son. When Theseus returned from Crete, after the death of the Minotaur, he omitted to hoist up white sails, as a signal of success, and at sight of black sails, Ægeus, concluding that his son was dead, threw himself into the sea, which, as some suppose, has since been called the Ægean Sea. Ægeus died B. C. 1235.

Æ'GIS. In Greek mythology, originally the skin of the goat Amalthea which suckled Zeus, and which skin was afterwards worn by him as part of his armor or as a covering of his shield; also the shield itself. In later times the Ægis was represented as part of the armor of Pallas Athena, and appears as a kind of breastplate covered with metal scales, and made terrible by the head of the Gorgon Medusa, being also fringed with serpents. The shield of Jupiter he gave to Pallas, who placed Medusa's head on it, which turned into stones all those who gazed at it.

Athena wearing the Ægis—From an antique statue.

AEL'LO, the name of one of the Harpies.

ÆGY'PTUS, son of Belus, and brother of Danaus, gave his fifty sons in marriage to the fifty daughters of his brother. Danaus, who had established himself at Argos and was jealous of his brother, obliged all his daughters to murder their husbands on the first night of their nuptials. This was done, Hypermnestra alone sparing her husband Lyneeus. Ægyptus himself was killed by his niece Polyxena.

ÆLIA'NUS CLAU'DIUS. A Roman sophist of Præneste in the reign of Adrian. He taught rhetoric at Rome. He wrote treatises on animals in seventeen books, and on various other subjects in fourteen books. Ælian died at the age of sixty, A. D. 140.

ÆNE'AS. A Trojan prince, son of Anchises and Venus. He married Creusa, the daughter of Priam, and they had a son named Ascanius. During the Trojan war Æneas behaved with great valor in defence of Troy. When the city was in flames he is said to have carried away his father Anchises on his shoulders, leading his son Ascanius by the hand, his wife following them. Subsequently he built a fleet of twenty ships, with which he set sail in quest of a settlement. He was driven on the coasts of Africa, and was kindly received by Dido, queen of Carthage, who became enamored of him; but he left Carthage by the order of the gods. After wandering about during several years, encountering numerous difficulties, he at length arrived in Italy, where he was hospitably received by Latinus, king of the Latins. After the death of Latinus, Æneas became king. He has been praised for his piety and his submission to the will of the gods; the term "Pius" is generally prefixed to his name. He is a hero of Homer's Iliad, and the great hero of Virgil's *Æneid*.

ÆNE'ID. An epic poem written by Virgil, of which Æneas, a Trojan, is the hero. It describes the taking of Troy by the Greeks, the subsequent wanderings of Æneas, and the final settlement of himself and companions in Italy.

ÆNE'IS. The Æneid, a grand poem by Virgil, the great merit of which is well known. The author has imitated the style of Homer, and is by some thought to equal him.

ÆOL'US, the ruler of storms and winds, was the son of Hippotas. He reigned over Æolia. He was the inventor of sails, and a great astronomer, from which the poets have called him the god of wind.

ÆS'CHINES. An Athenian orator who lived about 342 B. C. and distinguished himself by his rivalship with Demosthenes. Only three orations of his are extant.

ÆS'CHYLUS, a soldier and poet of Athens, son of Euphorion. He was in the Athenian army at the battles of Marathon, Salamis, and Platæa; but his most solid fame rests on his writings. He wrote seventy tragedies, forty of which were awarded with a public prize. He was killed by the fall of a tortoise, dropped from the beak of an eagle on his head, B. C. 456. Only seven of his tragedies are extant, the most celebrated being Prometheus.

Æscula'pius, son of Apollo and Coronis, or as some say of Apollo and Larissa, daughter of Phlegias, was the god of medicine. He married Epione, and they had two sons, famous for their skill in medicine, Machaon and Podalirus; of their four daughters, Hygeia, goddess of health, is the most celebrated.

Æ'son, son of Cretheus, was born at the same birth as Pelias. He succeeded his father in the kingdom of Iolchos, but was soon exiled by his brother. He married Aleimeda, by whom he had Jason, whose education he entrusted to Chiron. When Jason reached manhood he demanded his father's kingdom from his uncle, who gave him evasive answers, and persuaded him to go in quest of the Golden Fleece. On his return Jason found his father very infirm, and at his request Medea drew the blood from Æson's veins and refilled them with the juice of certain herbs, which restored the old man to the vigor of youth.

Æso'pus. A Phrygian philosopher who, originally a slave, procured his liberty by his genius. He dedicated his fables to his patron Crœsus. The fables which we have now under his name doubtless are a collection of fables and apologues of wits before and after the age of Æsop, conjointly with his own. He lived about B. C. 570.

Agamem'non, king of Mycenæ and Argos, was brother to Menelaus, and son of Plisthenes, the son of Atreus. He married Clytemnestra, and Menelaus Helen, both daughters of Tyndarus, king of Sparta. When Helen eloped with Paris, Agamemnon was elected commander-in-chief of the Grecian forces invading Troy. When before Troy he killed a stag sacred to Diana (Artemis) and to appease her consented to sacrifice his daughter Iphigenia.

Agesila'us. Of the family of Proclidæ, son of Archidamus, king of Sparta, whom he succeeded. He made war against Artaxerxes, king of Persia, with success, but in the midst of his conquests he was called home to oppose the Athenians and Bœotians. He passed over in thirty days that tract of country which had taken up a whole year of Xerxes' expedition. He defeated his enemies at Coronea, but sickness interfered with his conquests, and the Spartans were beaten in every engagement till he again appeared at their head. He died 362 years B. C.

AGRIC'OLA, a famous Roman pro consul of Britain, which he subdued. He died A. D. 93. His life has been written by the great Roman historian Tacitus.

AGRIP'PA, M. VIPSANIUS. A celebrated Roman who obtained a victory over S. Pompey, and favored the cause of Augustus at the battles of Actium and Philippi, where he behaved with great valor. In his expeditions in Gaul and Germany he obtained several victories, but refused the honor of a triumph, and turned his attention to the embelishment of Rome and the raising of magnificent buildings, amongst them the Pantheon. Augustus gave him his daughter Julia in marriage. He died universally lamented, at Rome, aged fifty-one, B. C. 12.

AGRIP'PA. A son of Aristobulus, grandson of the great Herod. He was popular with the Jews, and it is said that while they were flattering him with the appellation of god he was struck with death, A. D. 43. His son of the same name was with Titus at the siege of Jerusalem, and died A. D. 94. It was before him that St. Paul pleaded. There were a number of others of the same name, but of less celebrity.

A'JAX, son of Telamon and Peribœa, or Eribœa, was one of the bravest of the Greeks in the Trojan war. After the death of Achilles, Ajax and Ulysses both claimed the arms of the dead hero, which were given to Ulysses. Some say that he was killed in battle by Paris, but others record that he was murdered by Ulysses. (Iliad).

ALARI'CUS. A famous king of the Goths who plundered Rome in the reign of Honorius. He was greatly respected for his valor, and during his reign he kept the Roman empire in continual alarm. He died after a reign of twelve years, A. D. 410. He was buried in the bed of a river which had been turned from its course for the reception of his corpse, in order that it might be said that no one should tread on the earth where he reposed.

ALAS'TOR. A name of Jupiter (Zeus) as the avenger of evil.

AL'BION, son of Neptune and Amphitritite, came into Britain, where he established a kingdom, and introduced astrology and the art of building ships. Great Britain is called "Albion" after him.

ALCÆ'US. A celebrated lyric poet of Mitylene in Lesbos, about 600 years before the Christian era. He fled from a battle, and the armor in which he left the field was hung up in the temple of Minerva as a monument to his disgrace. He was enamored of Sappho. Of his works only a few fragments remain.

ALCES'TE or ALCES'TIS, daughter of Pelias, married Admetus. She, with her sisters, put her father to death that he might be restored to youth and vigor by Medea, who had promised to effect this by her enchantments. She, however, refused to fulfil her promise, on which the sisters fled to Admetus, who married Alceste.

ALCIBI'ADES An Athenian general, famous for his enterprise, versatile genius, and natural foibles. He was a disciple of Socrates, whose lessons and example checked for a while his vicious propensities. In the Peloponnesian war he encouraged the Athenians to undertake an expedition against Syracuse. He died in his forty-sixth year, B. C. 404.

ALCME'NA. Daughter of Electrion, king of Argos. Her father promised her and his crown to Amphitryon if he would revenge the death of his sons who had been killed by the Teleboans. In the absence of Amphitryon, Jupiter assumed his form and visited Alcmena, who, believing the god to be her lover, received him with joy. Amphitryon on his return ascertained from the prophet Tiresias the deception which had been practiced. After the death of Amphitryon Alcmena married Rhadamanthus. Hercules was the son of Jupiter and Alcmena.

ALCY'ONE or HALCY'ONE, daughter of Æolus, married Ceyx, who was drowned as he was going to consult the oracle. The gods apprised Alcyone in a dream of her husband's fate, and when she found his body washed ashore she threw herself into the sea, and she and her husband were changed into birds.

ALEC'TO. One of the Furies. She is represented with her

head covered with serpents, and breathing vengeance, war, and pestilence.

ALEC'TRYON, a servant of Mars, who was changed by him into a cock because he did not warn his master of the rising of the sun.

ALEXAN'DER, surnamed the Great, was son of Philip and Olympias. He was born B. C. 355, on the night on which the famous temple at Diana at Ephesus was burnt. This event, according to the magicians, was a prognostication of his future greatness, as well as the taming of Bucephalus, a horse which none of the king's attendants could manage. Philip, it is recorded, said, with tears in his eyes, that his son must seek another kingdom, as that of Macedonia would not be large enough for him. He built a town, which he called Alexandria, on the Nile. His conquests were extended to India, where he fought with Porus, a powerful king of the country, and after he had invaded Scythia he retired to Babylon, laden with spoils. His entry into the city was predicted by the magicians as to prove fatal to him. He died at Babylon in his thirty-second year, after a reign of twelve years and eight months of continual success, B. C. 323. There were a number of others of the same name, but of less celebrity.

ALCI'DES, one of the names of Hercules.

AL'FADUR, in Scandinavian Mythology the Supreme Being —Father of all.

AL'TAR. An elevated place on which sacrifices were offered or incense burned to a deity. The earliest altars were merely heaps of earth or turf or rough unhewn stone; but as the mode of sacrificing became more ceremonious grander altars were built. Some were of marble and brass, ornamented with carvings and bas-reliefs, and the corners with models of the heads of animals. They varied in height from two feet to four, and some were built solid; others were made hollow to retain the blood of the victims.

Ancient Altars.

Some were provided with a kind of dish, into which frankincense was thrown to overpower the smell of burning fat. This probably was the origin of the custom of burning incense at the altar. Greek and Roman altars were round, triangular, or square in form, often adorned with sculpture of the most tasteful and elaborate description, and bearing inscriptions. The Jews had the altar of burnt-offering, which stood at the entrance to the tabernacle, and afterwards occupied a corresponding site in the temple, and the altar of incense, which stood in the holy place.

ALTHÆ'A, daughter of Thestius and Eurythemis, married Œneus, king of Calydon, by whom she had many children, among them being Meleager. When he was born the Parcæ put a log of wood on the fire, saying, as long as it was preserved the life of the child would be prolonged. The mother took the wood from the flames and preserved it, but when Meleager killed his two uncles, Althæa, to revenge them, threw the log in the fire, and when it was burnt Meleager expired. Althæa then killed herself.

AMAL'THÆ'A, the goat which nourished Jupiter (Zeus).

AMARYL'LIS. The name of a country woman in Virgil's Eclogues. Some commentators have supposed that the poet spoke of Rome under this fictitious name.

AMAZ'ONES. A nation of famous women who lived near the river Thermodon in Cappadocia. All their lives were employed in wars and manly exercises. They founded an extensive empire in Asia Minor along the shores of the Euxine. Hercules totally defeated them, and gave Hippolyte, their queen, to Theseus for a wife. The race seems to have been exterminated after this battle.

AMBARVA'LIA were festivals in honor of Ceres, instituted by Roman husbandmen to purge their fields. At the spring festival the head of each

AMAZONS.
1, From Hope's Cost. of the Ancients.
2, From Museo Borbonico.

family led an animal, usually a pig or ram, decked with oak boughs, round his grounds, and offered milk and new wine. After harvest there was another festival, at which Ceres was presented with the first-fruits of the season. See Ceres.

AMBRA'CIA. A city of Epirus, the residence of King Pyrrhus. Augustus, after the battle of Actium, which resulted in the defeat of Antony and Cleopatra, called it Nicopolis. Lord Byron thus alludes to it in the second canto of "Childe Harold:"—

"Ambracia's gulf behold, where once was lost
A world for woman, lovely, harmless thing!

AM'MON. An ancient Ethiopian, and subsequently an Egyptian deity, called by the Greeks *Zeus Ammon*, and by the Latins *Jupiter Ammon*. Alexander the Great visited his temple in the desert of Libya, and was saluted, it is said, by the priests as son of the god.

AMPHIARA'US, son of Oicleus and Hypermnestra, was at the chase of the Calydonian boar, and accompanied the Argonauts in their expedition. He was famous for his knowledge of futurity.

Ammon, from a bronze in British Museum.

AMPHIC'TYON, son of Deucalion and Pyrrha, reigned at Athens after Cranaus. Some say the deluge happened in his age.

AMPHI'ON, son of Jupiter and Antiope. He cultivated poetry, and made such progress in music that he is said to have been the inventor of it, and to have built the walls of Thebes by the sound of his lyre. Husband of Niobe.

AMPHITRI'TE. A daughter of Oceanus and Tethys, who married Neptune (Poseidon). She was mother of Triton, a sea deity.

AMPHIT'RYON. A Theban Prince, son of Alcæus and Hipponome. His sister Anaxo married Electryon, king of Mycenæ, whose sons were killed in battle by the Teleboans. Electryon gave his daughter Alcmena to Amphitryon for avenging the death of his sons.

ANACHAR'SIS, a Scythian philosopher 592 years B. C., who,

on account of his wisdom, temperance, and knowledge, has been called one of the seven wise men. He has rendered himself famous among the Ancients by his writings, his poems on war, the laws of the Scythians, etc.

ANAC'REON. A famous lyric poet of Teos, in Ionia, favored by Polycrates and Hipparchus, son of Philostratus. He was of intemperate habits and fond of pleasure. Some of his odes are extant, and the elegance of his poetry has been the admiration of every age and country. He lived to the age of eighty-five, and after a life of voluptuousness was choked with a grape stone. He flourished B. C. 532.

ANADYOM'ENE. A famous painting by Apelles of Venus (Aphrodite) rising from the sea.

ANAXAG'ORAS. A Clazomenian philosopher, who disregarded wealth and honors to indulge his fondness for meditation and philosophy. He applied himself to astronomy, and obtained a knowledge of eclipses. He used to say he preferred a grain of wisdom to heaps of gold. He was accused of impiety and condemned to die, but he ridiculed the sentence, which he said had already been pronounced on him by nature. He died at the age of seventy-two, B. C. 428. He was the teacher of Euripides and Pericles.

ANAX'IMAN'DER, a Greek philosopher, died B. C. 547.

ANCHI'SES. A son of Capys and Themis. He was so beautiful that Venus came down from heaven on Mount Ida to enjoy his company. Æneas was the son of Anchises and Venus and was entrusted to the care of Chiron the Centaur. When Troy was taken, Anchises had become so infirm that Æneas had to carry him through the flames upon his shoulders, and thus saved his life.

ANLERS MARTI'US, fourth king of Rome, B. C. 640-616.

ANDROM'ACHE. Daughter of Eetion, king of Thebes. She married Hector, son of Priam, and was the mother of Astyanax. Her parting with Hector, who was going to battle, is described in the Iliad, and has been deemed one of the most beautiful passages in that great work. Pope's translation of the Iliad (book 6) describes with great pathos and beauty the parting of Hector from his wife and child. The passage is too long for quotation, but this quatrain from it shows the style:—

> "Thus having spoke, th' illustrous chief of Troy
> Stretch'd his fond arms to clasp the lovely boy;
> The babe clung crying to his nurse's breast,
> Scared at the dazzling helm and nodding crest."

ANDROM'EDA. A daughter of Cepheus, king of Æthiopia, and Cassiope. She was promised in marriage to Phineus when Neptune drowned the kingdom and sent a sea monster to ravage the country, because Cassiope had boasted that she was fairer than Juno and the Nereides. The oracle of Jupiter Ammon was consulted, but nothing could stop the resentment of Neptune except the exposure of Andromeda to the sea monster. She was accordingly tied to a rock, but at the moment that the monster was about to devour her, Perseus, returning from the conquest of the Gorgons, saw her, and was captivated with her beauty. He changed the monster into a rock by showing Medusa's head, and released Andromeda and married her.

ANEM'ONE. Venus changed Adonis into this flower.

ANGERO'NIA, otherwise Volupia, was the goddess who had the power of dispelling anguish of mind. Roman.

ANTÆ'US, a giant who was vanquished by Hercules. Each time that Hercules threw him the giant gained fresh strength from touching the earth, so Hercules lifted him off the ground and squeezed him to death.

AN'TEROS, one of the two Cupids, sons of Venus. Eros was the other.

ANTHROPOPH'AGI. A people of Scythia who fed on human flesh. They lived near the country of the Messagetæ. Shakspeare makes Othello, in his speech to the Senate, allude to the Anthropophagi thus:—

> "The cannibals that each other eat,
> The Anthropophagi, and men whose heads
> Do grow beneath their shoulders."

ANTIC'LEA, the mother of Ulysses, wife of Laertes.

ANTIG'ONE. A daughter of Œdipus, king of Thebes. She buried by night her brother Polynices, against the orders of Creon, who ordered her to be buried alive. She, however, killed herself on hearing of the sentence. The death of Antigone is the subject of one of the finest tragedies of Sophocles.

ANTIG'ONUS. One of Alexander's generals, who, on the division of the provinces after the king's death, received Pamphylia, Lycia, and Phrygia. Eventually his power became so great that Ptolemy, Seleucus, Cassander, and Lysimachus combined to destroy him. He gained many victories over them, but at last was killed in battle at the age of eighty, B. C. 301. There were others of the same name, but much less conspicuous.

ANTIN'OUS. A youth of Bithynia of whom the emperor Adrian was so extremely fond that, at his death, he erected a temple to him, and wished it to be believed that he had been changed into a constellation.

ANTI'OCHUS, surnamed *Soter*, was son of Seleucus and king of Syria. He made a treaty of alliance with Ptolemy Philadelphus, king of Egypt. He wedded his stepmother Stratonice. He was succeeded by his son Antiochus II., who put an end to the war which had begun with Ptolemy, and married his daughter Berenice, but being already married to Laodice, she, in revenge, poisoned him. Antiochus, the third of that name, surnamed the Great, was king of Syria, and reigned thirty-six years. He was defeated by Ptolemy Philopater at Raphia. He conquered the greater part of Greece, and Hannibal incited him to enter on a crusade against Rome. He was killed 187 years before the Christian era. Antiochus Epiphanes, the fourth of the name, was king of Syria after his brother Seleucus. He behaved with cruelty to the Jews. He reigned eleven years, and died unregretted. There were many others of the same name of less note.

ANTI'OPE, daughter of Nycteus, king of Thebes, and Polyxo, was beloved by Jupiter. Amphion and Tethua were her offspring.

ANTIP'ATER, son of Iolaus, was a soldier under King Philip, and raised to the rank of a general under Alexander the Great. When Alexander went to invade Asia, he left Antipater supreme governor of Macedonia. He has been suspected of giving poison to Alexander to advance himself in power.

Antoni′nus, surnamed Pius, was adopted by the Emperor Adrian, whom he succeeded. He was remarkable for all the virtues forming a perfect statesman, philosopher, and king. He treated his subjects with affability and humanity, and listened with patience to every complaint brought before him. He died in his seventy-fifth year, after a reign of twenty-three years, A. D. 160.

Anto′nius, Mar′cus, Mark Antony, the orator, distinguished himself by his ambitious views. When Julius Cæsar was killed in the senate house, Antony delivered an oration over his body, the eloquence of which is recorded in Shakspeare's tragedy of Julius Cæsar. Antony had married Fulvia, whom he repudiated to marry Octavia, the sister of Augustus. He fought by the side of Augustus at the battle of Philippi, against the murderers of Julius Cæsar. Subsequently he became enamored with Cleopatra, the renowned queen of Egypt, and repudiated Octavia to marry her. He was utterly defeated at the battle of Actium, and stabbed himself. He died in the fifty-sixth year of his age, B. C. 30.

Anto′nius, Ju′lius, son of the famous triumvir Antony, by Fulvia, was consul with Paulus Fabius Maximus. He was surnamed Africanus, and put to death by order of Augustus, but some say he killed himself.

Anto′nius, M. Gni′pho. A poet of Gaul who taught rhetoric at Rome. Cicero and other illustrious men frequented his school. There were a number of others of the same name, but of less repute.

Anu′bis. An Egyptian deity, the conductor of departed spirits, from this world to the next, represented by a human figure with the head of a jackal, and sometimes under the form of a jackal. He presided over tombs, and in the lower world he weighed the actions of the deceased previous to their admission to the presence of Osiris.

Anubis, from an Egyptian painting.

Apel′les. A celebrated painter of Cos, or, as others say, of Ephesus; son of Pithius. He lived in the age of Alexander the Great, who forbade any one but Apelles to paint his portrait. He was so absorbed in his profession that he never allowed a day to pass without employing himself at his art; hence the proverb, *Nulla dies sine linea*. His most perfect picture was Venus Anadyomene, which was not quite finished when he died. He painted a picture in which a horse was a prominent feature, and so correctly was it delineated that a horse passing by it neighed, supposing it to be alive. He was ordered by Alexander to paint a portrait of one of his favorites—Campaspe. Apelles became enamored with her and married her. He only put his name to three of his pictures—a sleeping Venus, Venus Anadyomene, and an Alexander.

APHRODI'TE. The Grecian name of Venus, from the Greek, meaning froth, because Venus is said to have been born from the froth of the ocean.

A'PIS. One of the ancient kings of Peloponnesus, son of Phoroneus and Ladodice. Some say that Apollo was his father, and that he was king of Argos, while others called him king of Sicyon, and fix the time of his reign above 200 years earlier. Varro and others have supposed that Apis went to Egypt with a colony of Greeks, and that he civilized the inhabitants and polished their manners, for which they made him a god after death, and paid divine honors to him under the name of Serapis.

A'PIS. A god of the Egyptians, worshipped under the form of an ox. Some say that Isis and Osiris are the deities worshipped under this name, because they taught the Egytians agriculture. Sometimes known as the bull of Memphis.

APPIA'NUS. An historian of Alexandria, who flourished A. D. 123. His Universal History, which consisted of twenty-four books, was a history of all the nations conquered by the Romans.

AP'PIUS CLAU'DIUS. A decemvir of Rome who obtained his power by force and oppression. He grossly insulted the maiden Virginia, whom her father killed to save her from the power of the tyrant.

APOL'LO. Son of Jupiter and Latona; called also Phœbus. He was known by several names, but principally by the following: Sol (the sun); Cynthius, from the mountain called Cynthus in the Isle of Delos, and this same island being his native place obtained for him the name of Delius; Delphinius, from his occasionally assuming the shape of a dolphin. His name was Delphicus, was derived from his connection with the splendid Temple of Delphi, where he uttered the famous oracles. Some writers record that this oracle became dumb when Jesus Christ was born. He was the god of the fine arts and the reputed originator of music, poetry, and eloquence. He had received from Jupiter the power of knowing futurity, and his oracles were in repute everywhere. As soon as he was born he destroyed with his arrows the serpent Python, which Juno had sent to persecute Latona; hence he was called Pythius. He was not the inventor of the lyre, as some have supposed, but it was given to him by Mercury, who received in return the famous Caduceus. He received the surnames of Phœbus, Delius, Cynthius, Pæan, Delphicus, etc. He is in sculpture generally represented as a handsome young man with a bow in his hand, from which an arrow has just been discharged.

Apollo, from a bas-relief at Rome.

APULIA, a district in the southeastern part of Italy.

ARCA'DIA. A district of Peloponnesus, which has been much extolled by the poets. It was famous for its mountains. The inhabitants were for the most part shepherds, who lived upon acorns. They were skilled warriors and able musicians. Pan lived chiefly among them.

ARCES'ILAUS. A Greek philosopher, the founder of the system of philosophy called the "New Academy." Flourished B. C. 250.

ARRCHIL'OCHUS. A lyric poet of Paros, who wrote elegies, satires, odes, and epigrams. He lived B. C. 685.

ARCHIME'DES. A famous geometrician of Syracuse who invented a machine of glass that represented the motion of the heavenly bodies. When Marcellus, the Roman consul, besieged Syracuse, Archimedes constructed machines which suddenly raised into the air the ships of the enemy, which then fell into the sea and were sunk. He also set fire to the ships with burning glasses. When the enemy were in possession of the town, a soldier, not knowing who he was, killed him, B. C. 212.

ARETHU'SA, a nymph of Elis, daughter of Oceanus, and one of Diana's attendants. As she returned one day from hunting, she bathed in the Alpheus stream. The god of the river was enamored of, and pursued her over the mountains, till Arethusa, ready to sink from fatigue, implored Diana to change her into a fountain, which the goddess did.

AR'GO. The name of the famous ship which carried Jason and his companions to Colchis, when they went to recover the Golden Fleece.

ARGONAU'TÆ. The Argonauts, those ancient heroes who went with Jason in the Argo to Colchis to recover the Golden Fleece, about seventy-nine years before the capture of Troy. The number of the Argonauts is not exactly known.

AR'GUS. A son of Arestor, whence he is sometimes called Arestorides. He had a hundred eyes, of which only two were asleep at one time. Juno set him to watch Io, whom Jupiter had changed into a heifer, but Mercury, by order of Jupiter, slew him, by lulling all his eyes to sleep with the notes of the lyre. Juno put the eyes of Argus in the tail of the peacock, a bird sacred to her.

ARIAD'NE, daughter of Minos, second king of Crete, and Pasiphæ, fell in love with Theseus, who was shut up in the labyrinth to be devoured by the Minotaur. She gave Theseus a clue of thread by which he extricated himself from the windings of the labyrinth. After he had conquered the Minotaur he married her, but after a time forsook her. On this, according to some authorities, she hanged herself. According to other writers, after being abandoned by Theseus, Bacchus loved her, and gave her a crown of seven stars, which were made a constellation.

ARI'ON. A famous lyric poet and musician, son of Cyclos of Methymna in Lesbos. He went into Italy with Periander, tyrant of Corinth, where he gained much wealth by his profession. Afterward he wished to revisit the place of his nativity, and he embarked in a ship, the sailors of which resolved to kill him for the riches he had with him. Arion entreated them to listen to his music, and as soon as he had finished playing he threw himself into the sea. A number of dolphins had been attracted by the sweetness of his music, and it is said that one of them carried him safely on its back to Tænarus, whence he went to the court of Periander, who ordered all the sailors to be crucified. Flourished about B. C. 625.

ARISTAR'CHUS. A celebrated grammarian of Samos, disciple of Aristophanes. He lived the greatest part of his life at Alexandria. He wrote about 800 commentaries on different authors. He died in his seventy-second year, B. C. 157. The greatest critic of antiquity.

ARISTI'DES. A celebrated Athenian, son of Lysimachus, in the age of Themistocles, whose great temperance and virtue procured for him the name of the "Just." He was rival to Themistocles, by whose influence he was banished for ten years, B. C. 448. He was at the battle of Salamis, and was appointed to be chief commander with Pausanias against Mardonius, whom they defeated at Platæa.

ARISTIP'PUS, the elder, a philosopher of Cyrene, a disciple of Socrates, and founder of the Cyrenaic sect.

ARISTOGI'TON and HARMO'DIUS. Two celebrated friends of Athens, who, by their joint efforts, delivered their country from the tyranny of the Pisistratidæ, B. C. 510.

ARISTOR. A stoic philosopher, B. C. 260.

ARISTOPH'ANES. A celebrated comic poet of Athens, son of Philip of Rhodes. He wrote fifty-four comedies, of which eleven have come down to us. He lived B. C. 434, and lashed the vices of the age with a masterly hand. The most celebrated of his works are "The Frogs," "The Clouds," and "The Birds."

ARISTOT'ELES. A famous philosopher, son of Nicomachus, born at Stagira. He went to Athens to hear Plato's lectures, where he soon signalized himself by his genius. He has been called by Plato the philosopher of truth, and Cicero complimented him for his eloquence, fecundity of thought, and universal knowledge. He died in his sixty-third year, B. C. 322. As he expired he is said to have exclaimed: *Causa causarum miserere mei*, which sentence has since become famous, and is by some attributed to Cicero. The term Stagirite has been applied to Aristotle from the name of his birthplace. He is often called "the greatest of the ancients."

ARMA'TA, one of the names of Venus, given to her by Spartan women.

AR'SACES. The founder of the Parthian empire.

ARTAXERX'ES the First succeeded to the kingdom of Persia after Xerxes. He made war against the Bactrians, and reconquered Egypt, which had revolted. He was remarkable for his equity and moderation.

ARTAXERX'ES the Second. King of Persia, surnamed Mnemon. His brother Cyrus endeavored to make himself king in his place, and marched against his brother at the head of 100,000 Barbarians and 13,000 Greeks. He was opposed by Artaxerxes with a large army, and a bloody battle was fought at Cunaxa, in which Cyrus was killed and his forces routed.

AR'TEMIS. The Greek name of Diana. Her festivals, called Artemesia, were celebrated in several parts of Greece, particularly at Delphi. She was one of the most favorite deities of the Greeks.

ARUS'PICES, sacrificial priests.

ASCAL'APHUS was changed into an owl, the harbinger of misfortune, by Ceres, because he informed Pluto that Proserpine had partaken of food in the infernal regions, and thus prevented her return to earth.

ASCA'NIUS, son of Æneas and Creusa, was saved from the flames of Troy by his father, whom he accompanied in his voyage to Italy. He was afterwards called Iulus. The Julian family of Rome traced their descent from him.

ASCOLIA, Bacchanalian feasts, from a Greek word meaning a leather bottle. The bottles were used in the games to jump on.

Aso'pus. A son of Jupiter, who was killed by one of his father's thunderbolts.

Aspa'sia. Daughter of Axiochus, born at Miletus. She came to Athens, where she taught eloquence. Socrates was one of her scholars. She so captivated Pericles by her accomplishments that he made her his companion. The conduct of Pericles and Aspasia greatly corrupted the morals of the Athenians, and caused much dissipation in the State.

Assy'na. A large district of Western Asia on the eastern shore of river Tigris.

Astar'te. A powerful divinity of Syria, the same as the Venus of the Greeks. She had a famous temple at Hierapolis in Syria, which was attended by 300 priests.

Astræ'a. A daughter of Astræus, king of Arcadia, or, according to others, daughter of Titan and Aurora. Some make her daughter of Jupiter and Themis. She was called Justice, of which virtue she was the goddess.

Asty'anax. A son of Hector and Andromache. He was very young when the Greeks besieged Troy, and when the city was taken his mother saved him in her arms from the flames. According to Euripides he was killed by Menelaus.

Atalan'ta. Daughter of Schœneus, king Scyros. According to some she was the daughter of Jasus, or Jasius, and Clymene, but others say that Menalion was her father. She determined to live in celibacy, but her beauty gained her many admirers, and to free herself from their importunities she proposed to run a race with them. As she was almost invincible in running, her suitors, who entered the lists against her, were defeated, till Milanion, the son of Macareus proposed himself as an admirer. Venus gave him three golden apples from the garden of the Hesperides, and with these concealed about him he entered the lists to race against Atalanta. As the race proceeded he dropped the apples, which she stopped to pick up, thus enabling Milanion to arrive first at the goal, and obtain her in marriage.

A'te. Daughter of Jupiter, and goddess of all evil. She raised such a discord among the gods that Jupiter banished her from heaven, and sent her to dwell on earth, where she incited mankind to evil thoughts and actions.

ATHENE (Minerva). A great deity of the Greeks. She sprang into life full grown from the head of Jupiter. The goddess of wisdom and power, the protectress of agriculture.

ATHANA'SIUS. A bishop of Alexandria, celebrated for his determined opposition to Arius and his doctrines. He died A. D. 373, after filling the archiepiscopal chair for forty-seven years. The famous creed which is named after him is no longer supposed to have been written by him, and its authorship remains in doubt.

AT'LAS. One of the Titans, son of Iapetus and Clymene. He married Pleione, daughter of Oceanus (or of Hesperis according to some writers.) He had seven daughters by his wife Pleione, they were called by one common name, Pleiades; and by his wife Æthra he had seven more, who were, in the same manner, called Hyades. Both the Pleiades and the Hyades are celestial constellations. He was also a great astronomer. He is depicted with the globe on his back, his name signifying great toil or labor. For his inhospitality to Perseus that king changed him into the mountain which bears his name of Atlas. A chain of mountains in Africa is called after him, and so is the Atlantic Ocean.

A'TREUS. A son of Pelops and Hippodamia, was king of Mycenæ. His brother Chrysippus was illegitimate, and Hippodamia wished to get rid of him, and urged Atreus and another of her sons, Thyestes, to murder him, which, on their refusal, she did herself. Atreus retired to the court of Eurystheus, king of Argos, and succeded to his throne.

ATTI'CA. The district of Greece ruled by Athena.

AT'TICUS, T. POMPONIUS. A celebrated Roman knight, to whom Cicero wrote a number of letters, containing the general history of the age. He retired to Athens, where he endeared himself to the citizens, who erected statues to him in commemoration of his virtues. He died at the age of seventy-seven B. C. 32.

AT'TILLA. A celebrated king of the Huns, who invaded the

Roman empire in the reign of Valentinian, with an army of half a million of men. He laid waste the provinces, and marched on Rome, but retreated on being paid a large sum of money. He called himself the "Scourge of God," and died A. D. 453, of an effusion of blood, on the night of his marriage.

AUG'ÆAS, a king of Elis, the owner of the stable which Hercules cleansed after three thousand oxen had been kept in it for thirty years. It was cleansed by turning the river Alpheus through it. Augæas promised to give Hercules a tenth part of his cattle for his trouble, but for neglecting to keep his promise, Hercules killed him.

AUG'UR. Among the ancient Romans a functionary whose duty was to derive signs concerning future events from the singing, chattering, and flight of birds, from the feeding of the sacred fowls, from certain appearances in quadrupeds, from lightning, and other unusual occurrences. There was a college or community of Augurs, originally three in number, and afterwards nine—four patricians and five plebeians. In the engraving the figure holds in the right hand the lituus or crooked staff of the Augur, and at its foot one of the sacred fowls.

Cæsar as an Augur From a Roman bas-relief.

AUGUS'TUS, OCTAVIA'NUS CÆ'SAR, first emperor of Rome, was son of Octavius, a senator, and Accia, sister of Julius Cæsar. He was associated in the triumvirate with Antony and Lepidus, and defeated the armies of Brutus and Cassius at Philippi. Octavia, the sister of Augustus, married Antony after the death of his wife Fulvia. Octavia, however, was slighted for the charms of Cleopatra, which incensed Augustus, who took up arms to avenge the wrongs of his sister, and at the great battle of Actium (B. C. 31), the forces of Antony and Cleopatra suffered a disastrous defeat. Augustus ruled Rome from 12 B. C. to 14 A. D., and died at the age of 76.

AURELIA'NUS, emperor of Rome, was austere and cruel in

the execution of the laws and in his treatment of his soldiers. He was famous for his military character, and his expedition against Zenobia, queen of Palmyra, gained him great honors. It is said that in his various battles he killed 800 men with his own hand. He was assassinated near Byzantium, A. D. 275.

AURE'LIUS, M. ANTONI'NUS, surnamed "the philosopher," possessed all the virtues which should adorn the character of a prince. He raised to the imperial dignity his brother, L. Verus, whose dissipation and voluptuousness were as conspicuous as the moderation of the philosopher. During their reign, the Quadi, Parthians and Marcomanni were defeated. Verus died of apoplexy, and Antoninus survived him eight years, dying in his sixty-first year, after a reign of nineteen years and ten days. His philosophic "Meditations," in 12 books, are extant.

AURO'RA. A goddess, daughter of Hyperion and Thia, or Thea. She is generally represented by the poets as sitting in a chariot and opening with her fingers the gates of the east, pouring dew on the earth, and making the flowers grow. The Greeks call her Eos.

B

BA'AL, a god of the Phœnicians.

BAB'YLON. A city in Asia on the Euphrates river, the capital of the ancient Babylonian empire.

BAC'CHANTES. The priestesses of Bacchus.

BAC'CHANTE. A priestess of Bacchus, or one who joined in the celebration of the feasts of Bacchus. One in a state of bacchic frenzy. The figure represents a Bacchante with cymbals.

Bacchante, from a marble in British Museum.

BAC'CHUS (Dionysus) was son of Jupiter and Semele, the daughter of Cadmus. He was the god of wine, and is said to have married Ariadne after she had been forsaken by Theseus. He is represented with a round, soft, and graceful form, approaching that of a maiden, frequently in an easy attitude and supporting himself by his thyrsus as if slightly intoxicated, with a languid countenance, and with his hair knit behind in a knot and wreathed with sprigs of ivy and vine leaves. He is said first to have taught the cultivation of the grape, and the preparation of wine and other intoxicating liquors.

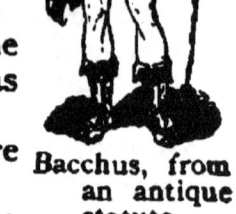

Bacchus, from an antique statute.

BA'LIOS. A famous horse given by Neptune to Peleus as a wedding present, and was afterwards given to Achilles.

BASSAR'IDES. The priestesses of Bacchus were sometimes so called.

BELISA'RIUS. A celebrated general who, in the reign of Justinian, emperor of Constantinople, renewed the victories which had rendered the first Romans so distinguished. He died, after a life of glory, suffering from royal ingratitude, 565 years before the Christian era.

BELLER'OPHON, son of Glaucus, king of Ephyre, and Eurymede, was at first called Hipponous. He was sent by Iobates, king of Lycia, to conquer the monster Chimæra. Minerva assisted him in the expedition, and by the aid of the winged horse Pegasus he conquered the monster and returned victorious. After sending him on other dangerous adventures, Iobates gave him his daughter in marriage and made him successor to his throne.

BELLO'NA, Roman goddess of war, was daughter of Phorcys and Ceto; called by the Greeks Enyo, and is often confounded with Minerva. She prepared the chariot of Mars when he was going to war, and appeared in battles armed with a whip to animate the combatants, and holding a torch.

BE'LUS, one of the most ancient kings of Babylon about 1800 years before the age of Semiramis, was made a god after death, and was worshipped by the Assyrians and Babylonians. He was supposed to be the son of the Osiris of the Egyptians. The temple of Belus was the most ancient and magnificent in the world, and was said to have been originally the tower of Babel.

BERECYN'THIA, a name of Cybele, from a mountain where she was worshipped.

BERENI'CE. A daughter of Philadelphus, who maried Antiochus, king of Syria, after he had divorced his former wife Laodice.

BERENI'CE. The mother of Agrippa, whose name occurs in the history of the Jews as daughter-in-law of Herod the Great. A number of others of minor celebrity were known by the same name.

BI'ON. A philosopher of Scythia who rendered himself famous for his knowledge of poetry, music and philosophy. Another of the same name was a Greek poet of Smyrna who wrote pastorals. He was a friend of Moschus, who says that he died by poison about 300 years B. C.

BITHY'NIA, a district of Asia Minor.

BOADICE'A. A famous British queen who rebelled against the Romans and was defeated, on which she poisoned herself. Her cruel treatment by the Romans is the subject of an ode by Cowper.

BŒO'TIA, a district of northern central Greece.

BOE'THIUS, a Roman author A. D. 470. He translated a commutal upon the great Greek philosopher.

BO'REAS. The name of the north wind blowing from the Hyperborean mountains. According to the poets, he was son of Astræus and Aurora. He was passionately fond of Hyacinthus.

BRAH'MAN. Among the Hindus one of the sacred or sacerdotal caste, who claim to have proceeded from the mouth of Brahma, the seat of wisdom, and to be the sole depositaries and interpreters of the Vedas. There are seven subdivisions of his caste, originating with seven penitents of high antiquity. Theoretically the Brahmans venerated equally the three gods or persons of the Hindu trimurti or trinity, but practically, the worship of Brahma having fallen into desuetude, they are divided into two sects—the devotees of Vishnu and those of Siva, the former wearing an orange-colored dress with the *nama*, or mark of the trident of Vishnu on the forehead, the latter being distinguished by the *lingam*, or emblem of the male organ of generation, and affecting greater abstemiousness. The Brahman passes through four states. He enters on the first stage at seven years of age. In it he learns to read and write, studies the Vedas, and makes himself familiar with the privileges of his caste, as his right to ask alms and to be exempted from taxes, as well as from corporal and capital punishment. The second state begins with his marriage, when regular ablutions, fasting, and many minute observances become incumbent upon him. In the third he retires to the forest, feeds upon herbs, roots, and fruits, bathes morning, noon, and evening, and subjects himself to the most rigorous penance. In the fourth state, which is that of penance, he suppresses his breath, stands upon his head, and performs other like painful ceremonies till he rises to a participation of the divine nature. Called also *Brahmin*.

BRAH'MA. One of the deities of the Hindoo trimurti or triad. He is termed the Creator, or the grandfather of gods and men; his brothers Vishnu and Siva being respectively the preserver and the destroyer. Brahma is usually represented as a red or golden-colored figure with four heads and four arms, and he is frequently attended by his vehicle the goose or swan. Brahma has long since ceased to occupy the high place he once held among the gods of India, and is seldom if at all worshipped, as, since the creation of the world, he has ceased to have any functions to perform. It will not be till the tenth *avatar* or incarnation (when the world will undergo total annihilation) that his services will be again put into requisition.

Brahma, from an idol in the Indian Museum.

BREN'NUS. A general of the Galli Senones, who entered Italy, defeated the Romans, and marched into the city.

The Romans fled into the Capitol, and left the city in possession of the enemy. The Gauls climbed the Tarpeian rock in the night, and would have taken the Capitol had not the Romans been awakened by the cackling of some geese, on which they roused themselves and repelled the enemy.

BRI'A'REUS. A famous giant, son of the Cœlus and Terra. He had a hundred hands and fifty heads, and was called by men by the name of Ægeon.

BRU'TUS, L. JUNIUS. Son of M. Junius and Tarquinia. When Lucretia killed herself B. C. 509, in consequence of the brutality of Tarquin, Brutus snatched the dagger from the wound and swore upon the reeking blade immortal hatred to the royal family, and made the people swear they would submit no longer to the kingly authority. His sons conspired to restore the Tarquins, and were tried and condemned before their father, who himself attended their execution.

BRU'TUS, MAR'CUS JU'NIUS, the destroyer of Cæsar, conspired, with many of the most illustrious citizens of Rome, against Cæsar, and stabbed him in Pompey's Basilica. The tumult following the murder was great, but the conspirators fled to the Capitol, and by proclaiming freedom and liberty to the populace, for the time established tranquility. Antony, however, soon obtained the popular ear, and the murderers were obliged to leave Rome. Brutus retired into Greece, where he gained many friends. He was soon pursued by Antony, who was accompanied by the young Octavius. The famous battle of Philippi followed, in which Brutus and his friend Cassius, who commanded the left wing of the army, were totally defeated. Brutus fell on his own sword, B. C. 42, and was honored with a magnificent funeral by Antony. Plutarch relates that Cæsar's ghost appeared to Brutus in his tent before the battle of Philippi warning him of his approaching fall.

BUCEPH'ALUS. A horse of Alexander's, so frequently named by writers that the term has become proverbial. Alexander was the only person who could mount him, and he always knelt down for his master to bestride him.

BUD'DHA. The Wise or the Enlightened; the sacred name of the founder of Buddhism, who appears to have lived in the sixth century B. C. One of the most prominent doctrines of his religious system is that *nirvana*, or an absolute release from existence, is the chief good. According to it pain is inseparable from existence, and consequently pain can cease only through nirvana; and in order to attain nirvana our desires and passions must be suppressed, the most extreme self-renunciation practiced, and we must, as far as possible forget our own personality. From Buddhism involving a protest against caste distinctions it was eagerly adopted by the Dasyus or non-Aryan inhabitants of Hindustan. It was pure, moral, and humane in its origin, but it came subsequently to be mixed up with idolatrous worship of its founder.

Buddha, from a Burmese Bronze.

C

CAC'ODÆ'MON. Greek name of an evil spirit.

CA'CUS, a famous robber, son of Vulcan and Medusa, represented as a three-headed monster vomiting flames. He resided in Italy, and the avenues of his cave were covered with human bones. When Hercules returned from the conquest of Geryon, Cacus stole some of his cows, which Hercules discovering, he strangled Cacus.

CAD'MUS, son of Agenor, king of Phœnicia, and Telephassa, or Agriope, was ordered by his father to go in quest of his sister Europa, whom Jupiter had carried away. His search proving fruitless, he consulted the oracle of Apollo, and was told to build a city where he saw a heifer stop in the grass, and call the country around Bœotia. He found the heifer, as indicated by the oracle. Requiring water, he sent his companions to fetch some from a neighboring grove. The water was guarded by a dragon, who devoured those who were sent for it, and Cadmus, tired of waiting, went himself to the place. He attacked the dragon and killed it, sowing its teeth in the ground, on which a number of armed men rose out of the earth. Cadmus threw a stone among them, and they at once began fighting, and all were killed except five, who assisted him in building the city. Cadmus introduced the use of letters in Greece—the alphabet, as introduced by him, consisting of sixteen letters.

CADU'CEUS. A rod entwined at one end with two serpents. It was the attribute of Mercury (Hermes), and was given to him by Apollo in exchange for the lyre.

CÆ'SAR. A surname given to the Julian family in Rome. This name, after it had been dignified in the person of Julius Cæsar and his successors, was given to the apparent heir of the empire in the age of the Roman emperors. The first twelve emperors were distinguished by the name of Cæsar. They reigned in this order: Julius Cæsar, Augustus, Tiberius, Caligula, Claudius, Nero, Galba, Otho, Vitellius, Vespasian, Titus and Domitian. Suetonius has written an exhaustive history of the Cæsars. C. Julius Cæsar, the first emperor of Rome, was son of L. Cæsar and Aurelia, the daughter of Cotta. He was descended, according to some accounts, from Julus, the son of Æneas. His eloquence procured him friends at Rome, and the generous manner in which he lived equally served to promote his interest. He was appointed for five years over the Gauls. Here he enlarged the boundaries of the Roman empire by conquest, and invaded Britain, which till then was unknown to the Romans. The corrupt state of the Roman senate, and the ambition of Cæsar and Pompey, caused a civil war. Neither of these celebrated Romans would endure a superior, and the smallest matters were grounds enough for unsheathing the sword. By the influence of Pompey a decree was passed to strip Cæsar of his power. Antony, as tribune, opposed this, and went to Cæsar's camp with the news. On this Cæsar crossed the Rubicon, which was the boundary of his province. The passage of the Rubicon was a declaration of war, and Cæsar entered Italy with his army. Upon this Pompey left Rome and retired to Dyrrachium, and Cæsar shortly afterwards entered Rome.

He then went to Spain, where he conquered the partisans of Pompey, and on his return to Rome was declared dictator, and soon afterwards consul. The two hostile generals met in the plains of Pharsalia, and a great battle ensued, B. C. 48. Pompey was defeated, and fled to Egypt, where he was slain. At length Cæsar's glory came to an end. Enemies had sprung up around him, and a conspiracy, consisting of many influential Romans, was formed against him. Conspicuous among the conspirators was Brutus, his most intimate friend, who, with others, assassinated him in the senate house in the ides of March, B. C. 44, in the fifty-sixth year of his age. He wrote his Commentaries on the Gallic wars when the battles were fought. This work is admired for its elegance and purity of style. It was after his conquest over Pharnaces, king of Pontus, that he made use of the words, which have since become proverbial, *Veni, vidi, vici*, illustrative of the activity of his operations.

CALIG'ULA, a Roman emperor, was son of Germanicus by Agrippina. He was proud, wanton and cruel. He was pleased when disasters befell his subjects, and often expressed a wish that the Romans had but one head that he might have the pleasure of striking it off. He had a favorite horse made consul, and adorned it with the most valuable trappings and ornaments. The tyrant was murdered A. D. 41, in his twenty-ninth year, after a reign of three years and ten months.

CALYP'SO. One of the Oceanides, or one of the daughters of Atlas, according to some writers. When Ulysses was shipwrecked on her coasts she received him with hospitality, and offered him immortality if he would remain with her as a husband, which he refused to do, and after seven years' delay he was permitted to depart from the island where Calypso reigned.

CAMIL'LUS, a name of Mercury, from his office of minister to the gods.

CALLIS'TRO. An Arcadian nymph, who was turned into a she-bear by Jupiter. In that form she was hunted by her son Arcas, who would have killed her had not Jupiter turned him into a he-bear. The nymph and her son form the constellations known as the Great Bear and Little Bear.

CALLI'OPE. One of the Muses, daughter of Jupiter and Mnemosyne, who presided over eloquence and heroic poetry.

CAL'YDON. A city of Ætolia, where Œneus the father of Meleager, reigned. During the reign of Œdneus, Diana sent a wild boar to ravage the country on account of the neglect which had been shown of her divinity by the king. All the princes of the age assembled to hunt the Calydonian boar. Meleager killed the animal, and gave the head to Atalanta, of whom he was enamored.

Calliope, from an antique statute in Vatican.

CA'MA. The Indian god of love and marriage.

CAMBY'SES, king of Persia, was the son of Cyrus the Great. He conquered Egypt, and was so disgusted at the superstition of the Egyptians that he killed their god Apis and plundered their temples.

CAMIL'LUS L. FU'RIUS. A celebrated Roman, called a second Romulus from the services he rendered his country. He was banished for distributing the spoils he had obtained at Veii. During his exile Rome was besieged by the Gauls under Brennus. The beseiged Romans then elected him dictator, and he went to the relief of his country, which he delivered after it had been some time occupied by the enemy. He died B. C. 365.

CAM'PUS MAR'TIUS. A large plain without the walls of Rome, where the Roman youth were instructed in athletic exercises, and learned to throw the discus, hurl the javelin, etc.

CAN'ACHE. The name of one of Actæon's hounds.

CAN'NÆ. A village of Apuleia, where Hannibal defeated the Roman consuls Æmylius and Varro, B. C. 216.

CAPITOLI'NUM. A celebrated temple of Jupiter and citadel at Rome on the Tarpein rock.

CAPNA, The chief city of Campania S. E. of Rome

CARACAL'LA, son of the emperor Steptimius Severus, was notorious for his cruelties. He killed his brother Geta in his mother's arms, and attempted to destroy the writings of Aristotle. After a life made odious by his vices he was assassinated, A. D. 217, in the forty-third year of his age.

CANE'PHORUS. One of the bearers of the baskets containing the implements of sacrifice, in the processions of the Dionysia, Panathenea, and other ancient Grecian festivals, an office of honor much coveted by the virgins of antiquity.

CANO'BA. The Indian Apollo.

CANO'PUS. The Egyptian god of water, the conqueror of fire.

CAP'IS or CAP'ULA. A peculiar cup with ears, used in drinking the health of the deities.

CAP-TOLI'NUS. A name of Jupiter, from the Capitoline hill, on the top of which a temple was built and dedicated to him.

Canephorus, from terra-cotta in British Museum.

CARAC'TACUS. A king of the Britons, who was conquered by the Romans and taken prisoner to Rome.

CARTHA'GO. Carthage, a celebrated city of Africa, the rival of Rome, and for a long period the capital of the country, and mistress of Spain, Sicily, and Sardinia. The time of its foundation is unknown, but it seems to be agreed on that it was built by Dido about 869 years before the Christian era, or, according to some writers, 72 or 73 years before the foundation of Rome. It had reached its highest glory in the days of Hamilcar and Hannibal. The city was destroyed B. C. 149, it was rebuilt after an interval, and about 400 A. D. was the principal city of Africa.

CASSAN'DER, son of Antipater, made himself master of Macedonia after his father's death, where he reigned for eighteen years.

CASSAN'DRA, daughter of Priam and Hecuba, was passionately loved by Apollo, who promised to grant her whatever she might require, and she obtained from him the power of seeing into futurity. Some say she received the gift of prophecy, with her brother Helenus, by being placed when young one night in the temple of Apollo, where serpents were found wreathed round their bodies and licking their ears, which gave them the knowledge of futurity. She was allotted to Agamemnon in the division of the spoils of Troy, and was slain by Clytemnestra, Agamemnon's wife.

Cassiope'ia. The Ethiopian queen who set her beauty in comparison with that of the Nereides, who thereupon chained her to a rock and left her.

Cap'ri'pedes. Pan, the Egipans, the Satyrs, and Fauns, were so called from having goats' feet.

Caproti'na. A name of Juno.

Cas'sius, C. A celebrated Roman who became famous by being first quæstor to Crassus in his expedition against Parthia. He married Junia, the sister of Brutus, and joined Brutus in the conspiracy formed to assassinate Cæsar, after which he returned to Philippi with Brutus, and commanded one wing of the army in the famous battle fought there. On the defeat of his forces he ordered one of his freedmen to kill him, and he perished by the sword which had inflicted a wound on Cæsar. He was called by Brutus "The last of all the Romans."

Casta'lius Fons, or Casta'lia. A fountain of Parnassus sacred to the Muses.

Cast'or and Poll'ux were twin brothers, sons of Jupiter and Leda. Mercury carried them to Pallena, where they were educated. As soon as they arrived at manhood they embarked with Jason in quest of the Golden Fleece. In this expedition they evinced great courage. Pollux defeated and slew Amycus in the combat of the Cestus, and was afterwards considered to be the god and patron of boxing and wrestling. Castor distinguished himself in the management of horses.

Catili'na, L. Ser'gius, a celebrated Roman, descended from a noble family. When he had squandered his fortune he secretly meditated the ruin of his country, and conspired with many Romans as dissolute as himself to extirpate the senate, plunder the treasures, and set Rome on fire. This plot, known as the Catiline conspiracy, was unsuccessful. The history of it is written by Sallust. Catiline was killed in battle B. C. 63.

CA'TO, PORCIUS, called "the Censor," distinguished senator and consul of Rome; a bitter enemy of Carthage; died B. C. 149.

CA'TO, MAR'CUS, was great-grandson of the censor Cato. The early virtues that appeared in his childhood seemed to promise that he would become a great man. He was austere in his morals and a strict follower of the tenets of the Stoics. His fondness for candor was so great that his veracity became proverbial. In the Catilinian conspiracy he supported Cicero, and was the chief cause of the capital punishment which was inflicted on some of the conspirators. He stabbed himself after reading Plato's treatise on the immortality of the soul, B. C. 46, in the fifty-ninth year of his age.

CATUL'LUS, C., or Q. VALE'RIUS. A poet of Verona whose compositions are the offspring of a luxuriant imagination. He was acquainted with the most distinguished people of his age. He directed his satire against Cæsar, whose only revenge was to invite him to a sumptuous banquet.

CEL'SUS, a physician in the age of Tiberius, who wrote eight books on medicine, besides treatises on agriculture, rhetoric, and military affairs.

CENTAU'RI. A people of Thessaly, half men and half horses. They were the offspring of Centaurus and Stilbia. The Centaurs were probably a race that hunted wild cattle and lived almost constantly on horseback. The earliest notices of them in Greek literature, however, merely represent them as a race of wild and savage men inhabiting the mountains and forests of Thessaly, and it is not till later times that they appear as in the cut. The Centaur Cheiron was distinguished for his knowledge of medicine.

Centaur.–Antique statue in Vatican Museum.

CENTUM'VIRI. The members of a court of justice at Rome. Though originally 105 in number, they were known as Centumvirs, and this name they retained when they were increased to 180.

CERBE′RUS. The watch-dog of the infernal regions, the offspring of the giant Typhaon and the serpent-woman Echidna. According to Hesiod he had fifty heads, but according to other mythologists he had three only, with the tail of a serpent, and with serpents round his neck. He was placed at the entrance of the infernal regions to prevent the living from entering, and the inhabitants of the place from escaping.

Cerberus—antique bronze.

CHÆRONE′A. A city of Bœotia celebrated for a great battle fought there in which the Athenians were defeated by the Bœotians, B. C. 447, and for the victory which Philip of Macedonia obtained there over the confederate armies of the Thebans and Athenians, B. C. 338. It was the birthplace of Plutarch.

CE′RES, the goddess of corn and harvests, was daughter of Saturn and Vesta. She was the mother of Proserpine, who was carried away by Pluto while she was gathering flowers. The Romans celebrated in her honor the festival of the Cerealia. Ceres was always represented in full attire, her attributes being ears of corn and poppies, while on her head she wore a corn-measure, and her sacrifices consisted of pigs and cows.

CHARYB′DIS. A dangerous whirlpool on the coast of Sicily. Personified, it was supposed to have been a woman who plundered travelers, but was at last killed by Hercules. Scylla and Charybdis are generally spoken of together to represent alternative dangers.

Ceres—antique statue in Louvre.

CHE′MOS. The Moabitish god of war.

CHE′OPS. A king of Egypt, after Rhampsinitus, famous for building pyramids.

CHA'RON. A god of the infernal regions, son of Nox and Erebus, who conducted the souls of the dead in a boat over the river Styx and Acheron. "Charon's toll" was a coin put into the hands of the dead with which to pay the grim ferryman.

Charon and two Spirits of deceased Persons.

"From the dark mansions of the dead,
Where Charon with his lazy boat
Ferries o'er Lethe's sedgy moat."

CHIMÆ'RA. A celebrated monster which continually vomited flames. It was destroyed by Bellerophon. It had the head and breast of a lion, the body of a goat, and the tail of a serpent; supposed to represent a volcanic mountain in Lycia, whose top was the resort of lions, the middle that of goats, and the foot that of serpents. It used to vomit fire.

Chimæra—Lycian terracotta. British Museum.

. . . "And on the craggy top
Chimera dwells, with lion's face and mane,
A goat's rough body and a serpent's train."
                                    POPE.

CHI'RON. A centaur, half a man and half a horse, son of Philyra and Saturn. He was famous for his knowledge of music, medicine, and shooting, and taught mankind the use of plants and medicinal herbs.

CHRYSOS'TOM. A bishop of Constantinople who died A. D. 407. He was a great disciplinarian, and by severely lashing the vices of his age he made many enemies.

CIC'ERO, M. T., born at Arpinum, was son of a Roman knight and lineally descended from the ancient kings of the Sabines. In youth he displayed many abilities, and was taught philosophy by Philo, and law by Mutius Scævola. He applied himself with great diligence to the study of oratory, and was distinguished above all the speakers of his time in the Roman Forum. He signalized himself in opposing Catiline, whom he publicly accused of treason against the State, and whom he drove from the city. After a number of vicissitudes of fortune he was assassinated, B. C. 43, at the age of sixty-three. The greatest orator that Rome produced.

CINCINNA'TUS, L. Q. A celebrated Roman, who was informed as he plowed in the fields that the senate had chosen him to be dictator. On this he left the plow and repaired to the field of battle, where his countrymen were opposed by the Volsci and Æqui. He conquered the enemy, and entered Rome in triumph.

CIR'CE. A daughter of Sol and Perseis, celebrated for her knowledge of magic and venomous herbs. She was carried by her father to an island called Æaea. Ulysses on his return from the Trojan war visited her coasts, and his companions were changed, by her potions, into swine. Ulysses, who was fortified against enchantments by an herb which he had received from Mercury, demanded of Circe the restoration of his companions to their former shape; she complied with his wishes, and eventually permitted him to depart from her island.

CLAU'DIUS, T. DRUSUS, son of Drusus, became emperor of Rome after the death of Caligula. He went to Britain, and obtained a triumph for victories achieved by his generals. He suffered himself to be governed by favorites whose avarice plundered the State and distracted the provinces. He was poisoned by Agrippina, who wished to raise her son Nero to the throne.

CLEOPA'TRA, queen of Egypt, daughter of Ptolemy Auletes, was celebrated for her beauty. Antony became enamored of her and married her, ignoring his connection with Octavia, the sister of Augustus. He gave her the greatest part of the eastern provinces of the Roman empire. This caused a rupture between Augustus and Antony, and these two famous men met at Actium, when Cleopatra, by flying with sixty ships, ruined the battle for Antony, and he was defeated. Cleopatra destroyed herself by applying an asp to her breast.

CLYTEMNES'TRA. A daughter of Tyndarus, king of Sparta, and Leda, married Agamemnon, king of Argos, in whose absence in the Trojan war she misconducted herself with his cousin Ægysthus. On the return of Agamemnon Clytemnestra murdered him, as well as Cassandra, whom he had brought with him. After this Clytemnestra ascended the throne of Argos. In the meantime her son Orestes, after an absence of seven years, returned, resolved to avenge the death of his father Agamemnon. On an occasion when Ægysthus and Clytemnestra repaired to the Temple of Apollo, Orestes, with his friend Pylades, killed them.

CLI'O. The first of the Muses, daughter of Jupiter and Mnemosyne. She presided over history. She is usually represented with a scroll in her hand, and also sometimes with a case to keep MSS. in by her side.

CLOACI'NA. A goddess of Rome who presided over the Cloacæ, which were large recepticles for the filth of the whole city.

CLO'THO, the youngest of the three Parcæ, who were daughters of Jupiter and Themis, was supposed to preside over the moment of birth. She held the distaff in her hand and spun the thread of life.

Clio — antique statute, Villa Borghese, Rome.

CLYT'IA or CLYT'IE. A daughter of Oceanus and Tethys, beloved by Apollo. She was changed into a sunflower.

CNEPH. In Egyptian mythology the creator of the universe.

COCY'TUS, the river of Lamentation. One of the five rivers of the infernal regions.

"Infernal rivers that disgorge
Into a burning lake their baleful streams.
. . . Cocytus, named of lamentation loud,
Heard on the rueful stream." MILTON.

CO'CLES, P. HORATIUS. A celebrated Roman who alone opposed the whole army of Porsena at the head of a bridge while his companions were cutting off the communication with the other shore. When the bridge was destroyed, Cocles, though wounded by the darts of the enemy, leaped into the Tiber and swam across it, armed as he was. For his heroism a brazen statue was raised to him in the Temple of Vulcan. Macaulay, who has written a noble poem on this heroic deed of Horatius Cocles, says: "There are several versions of the story, and these versions differ from each other in points of no small importance." According to his version Horatius had two companions who stood by his side defending the bridge; these were Spurius Lartius and Herminius. The final quatrain of the poem records how—

"With weeping and with laughter
  Still is the story told,
How well Horatius kept the bridge,
  In the brave days of old."

Co'DRUS. The last king of Athens, son of Melanthus. When the Heraclidæ made war against Athens, the oracle said that the victory would be granted to that nation whose king was killed in battle. The Heraclidæ on hearing this gave orders to spare the life of Codrus, but the patriotic king disguised himself, and engaging with one of the enemy, was killed. The Athenians obtained the victory, and Codrus was regarded as the savior of his country.

CŒ'LUS or URA'NUS. An ancient deity supposed to be the father of Saturn, Oceanus, and Hyperion.

COL'CHIS or COL'CHOS. A country of Asia famous for the expedition of the Argonauts, and as being the birthplace of Meda.

COLLATI'NUS, L. TARQUIN'IUS. A nephew of Tarquin the Proud. He married Lucretia. He, with Brutus, drove the Tarquins from Rome.

COLOS'SUS. A celebrated brazen image at Rhodes, which was considered to be one of the seven wonders of the world.

COM'MODUS, L. AURE'LIUS ANTONI'NUS, son of M. Antoninus, succeeded his father in the Roman empire. He was naturally cruel and fond of indulging his licentious propensities. Desirous of being likened to Hercules, he adorned his shoulders with a lion's skin, and carried a knotted club in his hand. He fought with the gladiators, and boasted of his skill in killing wild beasts in the amphitheater. He was strangled by a wrestler in the thirty-first year of his age, A. D. 192.

Co'mus. The god of revelry, feasting and nocturnal amusements. He is represented as a drunken young man with a torch in his hand.

Con'cord. The symbol of Concord was two right hands joined, and a pomegranate.

Concor'dia. The goddess of peace and concord at Rome, to whom Camillus raised a temple in the Capitol. She is represented as holding a horn of plenty in one hand, and in the other a sceptre, from which fruit is sprouting forth.

Confu'cius. A Chinese philosopher, as much honored among his countrymen as if he had been a monarch. He died about 499 years B. C.

Co'non. A famous general of Athens, son of Timotheus. He was made governor of all the islands of the Athenians, and was defeated in a naval battle by Lysander. He defeated the Spartans near Cnidos, when Pisander, the enemy's admiral, was killed. He died in prison, B. C. 393.

Constan'tia. A grand-daughter of the great Constantine, who married the Emperor Gratian.

Constanti'nus, surnamed the Great from the greatness of his exploits, was son of Constantius. It is said that as he was going to fight against Maxentius, one of his rivals, he saw a cross in the sky with the inscription, *In hoc signo vince*. From this he became a convert to Christianity, ever after adopting a cross for his standard. He founded a city where old Byzantium formerly stood, and called it Constantinopolis. There he kept his court, and made it the rival of Rome in population and magnificence. He died, A. D. 337, after a reign of thirty-one years of the greatest glory.

Constan'tius Chlo'rus, son of Eutropius, and father of the great Constantine. He obtained victories in Britain and Germany. He became the colleague of Galerius on the abdication of Dioclesian, and died A. D. 306, bearing the reputation of being brave, humane and benevolent.

Con'sul. A magistrate at Rome with regal authority for the space of one year. There were two consuls, who were annually chosen in the Campus Martius. The first two were L. Jun. Brutus and L. Tarquinius Collatinus.

Con'sus. A name given to Neptune as being the god of counsel.

Cophe'tua. A legendary king of Africa, who disliked women, but ultimately fell in love with a "beggar-maid," as mentioned in *Romeo and Juliet*.

> " . . Cupid, he that shot so trim
> When King Cophetua loved the beggar-maid."
> Shakspeare.

Co'pia, the goddess of plenty.

Corin'na. A celebrated woman of Thebes, whose father was Archelodorus. It is said that she obtained a poetical prize five times against the competitorship of Pindar.

Coriola'nus. The surname of C. Martius, from his victory over Corioli. After a number of military exploits, and many services to his country, he was refused the consulship. He was banished, and went to the Volsci, where he met with a gracious reception from Tullus Aufidius, whom he advised to make war against Rome, marching with the Volsci as general. His approach alarmed the Romans, who sent his mother and wife to meet him and appease his resentment against his countrymen, which with difficulty they succeeded in doing. Shakspeare has made his history the subject of the tragedy of "Coriolanus," which concludes with the assassination of the hero by Tullus Aufidius and his attendants.

Corne'lia. A daughter of Scipio Africanus, famous for her learning and virtues, and as being the mother of the Gracchi, Tiberius and Caius Gracchus. Her husband was T. Sempronius Gracchus.

Coro'nis, was a consort of Apollo and mother of Æsculapius. Another Coronis was daughter of a king of Phocis, and was changed by Athena into a crow.

Coryban'tes were priests of Cybele. They obtained the name because they were in the habit of striking themselves in their dances.

Cory'don. A silly, love-sick swain mentioned by Virgil, in his eclogues.

Cory'thaix. A name given to Mars, meaning Shaker of the Helmet.

Cras'sus, M. Licin'ius. A celebrated Román, who by

educating slaves and selling them, became very wealthy. He was made consul with Pompey, and was afterwards censor, and formed one of the first triumvirates, his associates in it being Pompey and Cæsar. In the hope of enlarging his possessions he left Rome, crossed the Euphrates, and hastened to make himself master of Parthia. He was met by Surena the Parthian general, and in the battle which ensued 20,000 of the Romans were killed and 10,000 made prisoners. Crassus surrendered, and was put to death B. C. 53.

CRE'ON, king of Corinth, was son of Sisyphus. He promised his daughter Glauce to Jason, who had repudiated Medea. To revenge herself on her rival, Medea sent her a present of a dress covered with poison. Glauce put it on, and was siezed with sudden pain. Her body took fire, and she expired in the greatest agony. The house in which she was, was also consumed, and Creon and his family shared Glauce's fate.

CRE'ON, king of Thebes, whose territories were ravaged by the Sphinx. Creon offered his crown to any one who would explain the enigmas proposed by the Sphinx. Œdipus solved the riddles, and ascended the throne of Thebes.

CRŒ'SUS. The fifth and last of the Mermnadæ, who reigned in Lydia, was the son of Alyattes, and was considered the richest man in the world. His court was an asylum for learning, and Æsop, the famous fable writer, with other learned men, lived under his patronage. "As rich as Crœsus," has become a proverb.

CRIO-SPHINX. One of the three varieties of the Egyptian sphinx, characterized by having the head of a ram, as distinguished from the *andro-sphinx*.

Crio-sphinx.

CYB'ELE. A goddess, daughter of Cœlus and Terra, and wife of Saturn. She is supposed to be the same as Ceres, Rhea, Ops, Vesta, etc. According to Diodorus, she was the daughter of a Lydian prince. On her birth she was exposed on a mountain, where she was tended and fed by wild beasts, receiving the name of Cybele from the mountain where her life had been preserved.

Cu'pid, god of love, son of Jupiter and Venus, is represented as a winged infant, naked, armed with a bow and arrows. On gems and ornaments he is represented generally as amusing himself with some childish diversion. Cupid, like the rest of the gods, assumed different shapes, and we find him in the Æneid putting on, at the request of his mother, the form of Ascanius, and going to Dido's court, where he inspired the queen with love. He is generally represented as a beautiful child with wings, blind, and carrying a bow and quiver of arrows, with which he transpierced the hearts of lovers, inflaming them with desire.

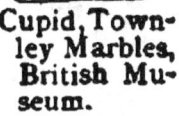
Cupid, Townley Marbles, British Museum.

Cur'tius, M. A Roman who devoted himself to the service of his country, about 360 years B. C., by leaping, on horseback and fully armed, into a huge gap in the earth at the command of the oracle.

Cy'clops. A race of men of gigantic stature, supposed to be the sons of Cœlus and Terra. They had only one eye, which was in the center of the forehead. According to Hesiod they were three in number, and named Arges, Brontes, and Steropes.

Cyg'nus, the bosom friend of Phæton. He died of grief on the death of his friend, and was turned into a swan.

Cyll'aros, one of Castor's horses. The color is mentioned as being coal-black, with white legs and tail.

Cyl'lo. The name of one of Actæon's hounds, which was lame.

Cyllop'otes. A name given to one of Actæon's hounds which limped.

Cyn'osure. One of the nurses of Jupiter, turned by the god into a conspicuous constellation.

Cyparis'sus. A boy of whom Apollo was very fond, and when he died he was changed, at Apollo's intercession, into a cypress tree, the branches of which typify mourning.

Cy'pria. A name of Venus, because she was worshipped in the island of Cyprus.

Cy'rus. A king of Persia, son of Cambyses and Mandane, daughter of Astyages, king of Media. Xenophon has written the life of Cyrus; and delineates him as a brave and virtuous prince, and often puts in his mouth many of the sayings of Socrates.

Cy'rus, the younger, was the son of Darius Nothus and the brother of Artaxerxes, the latter succeeding to the throne at the death of Nothus. Cyrus was appointed to the command of Lydia and the sea-coasts, where he fomented rebellion and levied troops under various pretences. At length he took the field with an army of 100,000 Barbarians and 13,000 Greeks under the command of Clearchus. Artaxerxes met him with 900,000 men near Cunaxa. The engagement ended fatally for Cyrus, who was killed 401 years B. C. He is always called Cyrus the Great.

Cyth'era. A name of Venus, from the island to which she was wafted in the shell.

D

Dacty'li were priests of Cybele. They were given the name, because, like the fingers, they were ten in number.

Dæd'alus, an Athenian, was the most ingenious artist of his age; he was the inventor of the wedge and many other mechanical instruments. He made a famous labyrinth for Minos, king of Crete, but incurred the displeasure of Minos, who ordered him to be confined in the labyrinth. Here he made himself wings with feathers and wax, and fitted them to his body, adopting the same course with his son Icarus who was the companion of his confinement. They mounted into the air, but the heat of the sun melted the wax on the wings of Icarus, and he fell into the ocean, which after him has been called the Icarian Sea. The father alighted safely at Cumæ, where he built a temple to Apollo.

Dan'ae, daughter of Acrisius, king of Argos, and Eurydice. Jupiter was enamored with her, and they had a son, with whom Danæ was exposed in a boat on the sea by her father. The winds carried them to the island of Seriphus, where she was saved by some fishermen, and carried to Polydectes, king of the place, whose brother, named Dictys, educated the child, who was called Perseus, and kindly treated the mother.

DA'GON. The national god of the Philistines, represented with the upper part of a man and the tail of a fish. His most famous temples were at Gaza and Ashdod. He had a female corelative among the Syrians. In Babylonian mythology, the name Dagon is given to a fish-like being who rose from the waters of the Red Sea as one of the great benefactors of men.

Dagon of the Philistines.

Dagon his name, sea-monster, upward man,
And downward fish.   MILTON.

DANA'IDES. The fifty daughters of Danaus, king of Argos, who married the fifty sons of their uncle Ægyptus. Danaus had been told by the oracle that he would be killed by a son-in-law, and he made his daughters promise to slay their husbands immediately after marriage. All of them fulfilled their father's wishes except one, Hypermnestra, who spared her husband Lynceus.

DAPH'NE. A daughter of the river Peneus, or of the Ladon, and the goddess Terra, of whom Apollo became enamored. Daphne fled to avoid the addresses of this god, and was changed into a laurel.

DAR'DANUS. A son of Jupiter, who killed his brother Jasius to obtain the kingdom of Etruria. He built the city of Dardania, and was reckoned to have been the founder of Troy.

DARI'US. A noble satrap of Persia, son of Hystaspes, who usurped the crown of Persia, after the death of Cambyses. Darius was twenty-nine years old when he ascended the throne, and he soon distinguished himself by his military prowess. He besieged Babylon, which he took after a siege of twenty months. He died B. C. 485.

DARI'US, the second king of Persia of that name, ascended the throne of Persia soon after the murder of Xerxes.

erals and the son of Cyrus the younger. He died B. C. 404, after a reign of nineteen years.

DARI'US. The third king of Persia of that name. He soon had to take the field against Alexander, who invaded Persia. Darius met him with an enormous army, which, however, was more remarkable for the luxuries indulged in by its leaders than for military courage. A battle was fought near the Granicus, in which the Persians were easily defeated, and another conflict followed near Issus, equally fatal to the Persians. Darius escaped and as- He carried on many wars with success, aided by his gen- sembled another powerful army. The last and decisive battle was fought at Arbela, Alexander being again victorious. When the fight was over Darius was found in his chariot covered with wounds and expiring, B. C. 331.

DEJANI'RA. A daughter of Œneus, king of Ætolia. Her beauty procured her many admirers, and her father promised to give her in marriage to him who should excel in a competition of strength. Hercules obtained the prize, and married Dejanira.

DEL'PHI. A town of Phocis at the southwest side of Mount Parnassus. It was famous for a temple of Apollo, and for an oracle celebrated in every age and country.

DE'MARUS. The Phœnician name of Jupiter.

DE'MOGOR'GON was the tyrant genius of the soil or earth, the life and support of plants. He was depicted as an old man covered with moss, and was said to live underground. He is sometimes called the king of the elves and fays.

DEME'TRIUS. A son of Antigonus and Stratonice, surnamed Poliorcetes, *destroyer of towns*. At the age of twenty-two he was sent by his father against Ptolemy, who had invaded Syria. He was defeated at Gaza, but soon afterwards obtained a victory. The greater part of his life was passed in warfare, his fortune undergoing many changes. He was distinguished for his fondness of dissipation when in dissolute society, and for military skill and valor on the battlefield. He died B. C. 286.

DEME'TRIUS. Surnamed *Soter*, king of Syria. His father gave him as a hostage to the Romans. After the death of his father, Seleucus Philopater, Antiochus Epiphanes usurped the throne of Syria, and was succeeded by his son Antiochus Eupator. Demetrius procured his liberty, and established himself on the throne, causing Eupator to be put to death.

DEME'TRIUS. Son of Soter, whom he succeeded after he had driven from the throne an usurper, Alexander Bala. Demetrius gave himself up to luxury, and suffered his kingdom to be governed by his favorites, thus becoming odious to his subjects. He was at last killed by the governor of Tyre, where he had fled for protection.

DEME'TRIUS PHALE'REUS. A disciple of Theophrastus, who gained such influence over the Athenians by his eloquence and the purity of his manners, that he was elected decennial archon, B. C. 317. He embellished the city, and rendered himself popular by his munificence, but his enemies plotted against him, and he fled to the court of Ptolemy Lagus, where he was received with kindness. He put an end to his life by permitting an asp to bite him, B. C. 284. There were several others of the name of Demetrius of minor note.

DEMOC'RITUS. A celebrated philosopher of Abdera, one of the disciples of Leucippus. He traveled over the greatest part of Europe, Asia, and Africa, in quest of knowledge, and returned home in the greatest poverty. He indulged in continual laughter at the follies of mankind for distracting themselves with care and anxiety in the short term of their lives. He told Darius, who was inconsolable for the loss of his wife, that he would raise her from the dead if he could find three persons who had gone through life without adversity, whose names he might engrave on the queen's monument. He taught his disciples that the soul died with the body. He died in his 109th year, B. C. 361. He has been termed "the laughing philosopher."

DEMOS'THENES, a celebrated Athenian, was the son of a rich blacksmith, and Cleobule. He became pupil of Plato, and applied himself to study the orations of Isocrates. At the age of seventeen he gave early proof of his eloquence and abilities in displaying them against his guardians, from whom he obtained restitution of the greater part of hi‹

estate. To correct the stammering of voice under which he labored he spoke with pebbles in his mouth. In the battle of Cheronæa he evinced cowardice, and saved his life by flight. He ended his life by taking poison, which he always carried in a quill, in the sixtieth year of his age B. C. 322. The greatest orator of Athens.

DEUCA′LION. A son of Prometheus, who married Pyrrha the daughter of Epimetheus. He reigned over part of Thessaly, and in his age the earth was covered by a deluge of water, sent by Jupiter as a punishment for the impiety of mankind. Deucalion constructed a ship, and by this means saved himself and Pyrrha. The ship, after being tossed on the waves for nine days, rested on Mount Parnassus. The deluge of Deucalion is supposed to have occurred B. C. 1503.

DIA′NA, The goddess of hunting. According to Cicero there were three of the name, viz:—a daughter of Jupiter and Proserpine, a daughter of Jupiter and Latona, and a daughter of Upis and Glauce. The second is the most celebrated, and all mention of Diana by ancient writers refers to her. To shun the society of men she devoted herself to hunting, and was always accompanied by a number of young women, who like herself, abjured marriage. She is represented with a quiver, and attended by dogs. The most famous of her temples was that at Ephesus, which was one of the wonders of the world.

Diana—Antique statute in the Louvre.

DI′DO. A daughter of Belus, king of Tyre, who married Sichæus or Sicharbus, her uncle, who was priest of Hercules. Pygmalion killed Sichæus to obtain his immense riches, and Dido, disconsolate at the loss of her husband, set sail with a number of Tyrians in quest of a place in which to form a settlement. A storm drove her fleet on the African coast, and she bought of the inhabitants as much land as could be covered by a bull's hide cut into thongs. On this land she built a citadel called Byrsa, which was the nucleus of a great city. Her subjects wished her to marry again, but she refused, and erected a funeral pile, on which she ascended and stabbed herself to death. (Virgil).

DIOCLETIA'NUS, CAI'US VALER'IUS JO'VIUS. A celebrated Roman emperor, born of an obscure family in Dalmatia. He was first a common soldier, and by merit gradually rose to the position of a general, and at length he was invested with imperial power. He has been celebrated for his military virtues, and though he was naturally unpolished by education, yet he was the friend and patron of learning and genius. His cruelty, however, against the followers of Christianity, has been severely reprobated. After reigning twenty-one years in great prosperity, he abdicated, A. D. 304, and died nine years afterwards, aged sixty-eight.

DIODO'RUS, SIC'ULUS. Celebrated as the author of a history of Egypt, Persia, Syria, Media, Greece, Rome, and Carthage. It was divided into forty books, of which only fifteen are extant, with a few fragments.

DIO'GENES. A celebrated cynic philosopher of Sinope, banished from his country for coining false money. From Sinope he retired to Athens, where he became the disciple of Antisthenes, who was at the head of the Cynics. He dressed himself in the garment which distinguished the Cynics, and walked about the streets with a tub on his head, which served him as a house. His singularity, joined to his great contempt for riches, gained him reputation, and Alexander the Great visited the philosopher and asked him if there was anything in which he could oblige him. "Get out of my sunshine," was the reply of the Cynic. Such independence pleased the monarch, who, turning to his courtiers, said: "Were I not Alexander, I would wish to be Diogenes.' He was once sold as a slave, and his magnanimity so pleased his master, that he made him the preceptor of his children and the guardian of his estates. He died B. C. 324, in the ninety-sixth year of his age. The life of Diogenes does not bear strict examination; while boasting of his poverty, he was so arrogant that it has been observed that his virtues arose from pride and vanity, not from wisdom or sound philosophy.

DIO'GENES LAER'TIUS. An Epicurean philosopher, born in Cilicia. He wrote the lives of the philosophers in ten books. This work contains an accurate account of the ancient philosophers, and is replete with anecdotes respecting them. It is compiled, however, without any plan, method, or precision, though neatness and conciseness are observable in it.

DIOME'DES, son of Tydeus and Delphyle, was king of Ætolia, and one of the bravest of the Grecian chiefs in the Trojan war. He often engaged Hector and Æneas, and obtained much military glory.

DIOME'DES. A king of Thrace, son of Mars and Cyrene, who fed his horses with human flesh. Hercules destroyed Diomedes, and gave him to his own horses to be devoured.

DI'ON. A Syracusan, son of Hipparina, famous for his power and abilities. He was related to Dionysius the First, who constantly advised with him, and at whose court he obtained great popularity. He was assassinated 354 years before the Christian era by one of his familiar friends. His death was greatly lamented by the Syracusans, who raised a monument to his memory. When Dionysius the Second ascended the throne he banished Dion, who collected some forces, and in three days made himself master of Syracuse.

DI'ON CAS'SIUS. A native of Nicæa in Bithynia, who was raised to some of the greatest offices of state in the Roman empire. He is celebrated as the writer of a history of Rome which occupied him twelve years in composing.

DIONYS'IUS the Elder was son of Hermocrates. He signalized himself in the wars which the Syracusans carried on against Carthage, and made himself absolute at Syracuse. His tyranny rendered him odius to his subjects. He made a subterraneous cave in a rock in the form of a human ear, which was called "the Ear of Dionysius." The sounds of this cave were all directed to one common tympanum, which had a communication with an adjoining room, where Dionysius spent part of his time in listening to what was said by those whom he had imprisoned. He died in the sixty-third year of his age, B. C. 368, after a reign of thirty-eight years.

DIONYS'IUS the Younger was son of Dionysius the First and Doris. He succeeded his father, and as soon as he ascended the throne he invited Plato to his court and studied under him for some time. Plato advised him to lay aside the supreme power, in which he was supported by Dion. This highly incensed Dionysius, who banished Dion, who collected forces in Greece, and in three days rendered himself master of Syracuse, and expelled the tyrant, B. C. 357. He, however, recovered Syracuse ten years afterwards, but was soon compelled to retire again by the Corinthians under Timoleon.

DIONYS'IUS of Halicarnassus. A historian who left his country and came to reside in Rome that he might study all the authors who had written Roman history. He was occupied during twenty-four years on his work on Roman antiquities, which consisted of twenty books.

DIR'CE. A woman whom Lycus, king of Thebes, married after he had divorced Antiope. Amphion and Zethus, sons of Antiope, for cruelties she practiced on Antiope, tied Dirce to the tail of a wild bull, by which she was dragged over rocks and precipices till the gods pitied her and changed her into a fountain.

DISCOR'DIA. A malevolent deity, daughter of Nox, and sister to Nemesis, the Parcæ, and Death. She was driven from heaven by Jupiter because she sowed dissensions among the gods. At the nuptials of Peleus and Thetis she threw an apple among the gods, inscribed with the words, *Detur pulchriori*, which was the primary cause of the ruin of Troy, and of infinite misfortunes to the Greeks.

DOLABEL'LA, P. CORN. A Roman who married the daughter of Cicero. During the civil wars he warmly espoused the cause of Julius Cæsar, whom he accompanied at the famous battle of Pharsalia and Munda.

DOMITIA'NUS, TI'TUS FLA'VIUS, son of Vespasian and Flavia Domitilla, made himself emperor of Rome on the death of his brother Titus, whom, according to some accounts, he destroyed by poison. The beginning of his reign promised hopefully, but Domitian became cruel, and gave way to vicious indulgences. In the latter part of his reign he became suspicious and remorseful. He was assassinated A. D. 96, in the forty-fifth year of his age.

DRA'CO. A celebrated lawgiver of Athens, who made a code of laws, B. C. 623, which on account of their severity, were said to be written in letters of blood. Hence the term "Draconic," applied to any punishment of exceptional severity.

DRU'SUS. A son of Tiberius and Vipsania, who became famous for his courage displayed in Illyricum and Pannonia.

DRU'SUS, M. LIV'IUS. A celebrated Roman, who renewed the proposals bearing on Agrarian laws, which had proved fatal to the Gracchi.

DRU'SUS, NERO CLAU'DIUS. A son of Tiberius Nero and Livia. He distinguished himself in the wars in Germany and Gaul, and was honored with a triumph. There were other Romans of the same name, but of smaller distinction.

DRY'ADES. Nymphs that presided over the woods. Oblations of milk, oil, and honey were offered to them. Sometimes the votaries of the Dryads sacrificed a goat to them.

DUR'GA. A Hindoo divinity; one of the names given to the consort of Siva, other names being Devi, Kali, Parvati, Bhavani, Uma, etc. She is the Amazon champion and protectress of the gods, and has been compared to the Hera (Juno), and the Pallas or armed Athene of the Greeks. She is generally represented with ten arms. In one hand she holds a spear, with which she is piercing Mahisha, the chief of the demons, the killing of whom was her most famous exploit; in another, a sword; in a third, the hair of the demon-chief, and the tail

Durga, from Coleman's Hindoo Mythology.

of a serpent twined round him; and in others, the trident, discus, ax, club, and shield, A great festival in her honor, the *durga puja*, is celebrated annually in Bengal, lasting for ten days.

DUUM'VIRI. Two patricians of Rome, first appointed by King Tarquin to keep the Sibylline books, which were supposed to contain the fate of the Roman empire.

E

E'ACUS, son of Jupiter and Egina, one of the judges of the infernal regions, who was appointed to judge the Europeans.

EB'LIS, the Mohammedan evil genius.

ECHID'NA. A woman having a serpent's tail. She was the reputed mother of Chimera, and also of the many-headed dog Orthos, of the three hundred headed dragon, of the Hesperides, of the Colchain dragon, of the Sphinx, of Cerberus, of Scylla, of the Gorgons, of the Lernæan Hydra, of the vulture that gnawed away the liver of Prometheus, and also the Nemean lion; in fact, the mother of all adversity and tribulation.

ECH'O. A daughter of the Air and Tellus, who was one of Juno's attendants. She was deprived of speech by Juno, but was allowed to reply to questions put to her.

EGEON. A giant sea-god, who assisted the Titans against Jupiter.

EGE'RIA. A nymph of Aricia in Italy, where Diana (Artemis) was particularly worshipped. Egeria was courted by Numa, and, according to Ovid, became his wife. Ovid says that she was disconsolate at the death of Numa, and that she wept so violently that Diana changed her into a fountain.

ELEC'TRA. A daughter of Agamemnon, king of Argos. She incited her brother Orestes to revenge his father's death by assassinating his mother Clytemnestra. Her adventures and misfortunes form the subject of one of the finest of the tragedies of Sophocles.

ELECTRY'ON. Son of Perseus and Andromeda, king of Mycenæ, father of Alcmene.

ELEUSIN'IA. A great festival observed by the Lacedæmonians, Cretans, and others, every fourth year, and by the people of Athens every fifth year, at Eleusis in Attica, where it was introduced by Eumolpus, B. C. 1356. It was the most celebrated of all the religious ceremonies of Greece. The term "Mysteries" is often applied to it. The expression "Eleusinian mysteries," as applied to anything that is inexplicable, has become proverbial.

ELYS'IUM. According to Virgil, the Elysian Fields, a place in the infernal regions, where, according to the ancients, the souls of the virtuous existed after death. Homer makes it a land in the west where the blessed live forever.

EMPED'OCLES. A philosopher, poet, and historian of Agrigentum in Sicily, who lived 444 B. C. He was a Pythagorean, and warmly espoused the belief in the transmigration of souls.

ENDYM'ION. A shepherd, son of Æthlius and Calyce. He is said to have required of Jupiter (Zeus) that he might be always young. Diana (Artemis) saw him as he slept on Mount Latmos, and was so struck with his beauty that she came down from heaven every night to visit him.

EN'NIUS, Q. An ancient poet, born in Calabria. He obtained the privileges of a Roman citizen on account of his learning and genius. He died B. C. 169.

E'OS. The name of Aurora among the Greeks.

EPAMINON'DAS. A famous Theban descended from the ancient kings of Bœotia. At the head of the Theban armies he defeated the Spartans at the celebrated battle of Leuctra about 370 B. C. He was killed in battle in the forty-eighth year of his age.

EPH'ESUS. A city of Ionia, famous for a temple of Diana, which was considered to be one of the seven wonders of the world.

EPH'IAL'TES. A giant who lost his right eye in an encounter with Hercules, and the left eye was destroyed by Apollo.

EPICTE'TUS. A Stoic philosopher of Hieropolis, originally the slave of Epaphroditus, the freedman of Nero. He supported the doctrine of the immortality of the soul.

EPICU'RUS. A celebrated philosopher, born in Attica of obscure parents. He distinguished himself at school by the brilliancy of his genius. He taught that the happiness of mankind consisted in pleasure, which arises from mental enjoyment, and the sweets of virtue. His death occured 270 B. C., his age being seventy-two.

ERATO. One of the Muses, whose name signifies loving or lovely. She presided over lyric and especially amatory poetry, and is generally represented crowned with roses and myrtle, and with the lyre in the left hand and the plectrum in the right in the act of playing.

ER'EBUS. A deity of the infernal regions, son of Chaos and Darkness. The poets often use the word to signify the infernal regions.

Erato, Antique, British Museum.

ERETOS'THENES. A celebrated scholar of Athens. He wrote on all the branches of knowledge cultivated in his day, especially grammar and astronomy. He died of voluntary starvation B. C. 196.

ERGA'TIS. A name given to Minerva. It means the work-woman, and was given to the goddess because she was credited with having invented spinning and weaving.

ERIC'THEUS, fourth King of Athens, was the son of Vulcan (Hephæstus).

ERIN'NYS. A Greek name of the Furies. It means Disturber of the Mind.

ERISICH'THON was punished with perpetual hunger because he defiled the groves of Ceres, and cut down one of the sacred oaks.

ER'IS. The goddess of discord, the sister of Mars (Ares). In latin she is known as Discordia.

ER'OS. The Greek god of love. In latin Amor

EROS'TRATUS. The rascal who burnt the temple of Diana at Ephesus, thereby hoping to make his name immortal.

ERYC'INA. A name of Venus, from Mount Eryx in Sicily.

ERYTHRE'OS. The Grecian name of one of the horses of Sol's chariot.

E'THON. One of the horses who drew the chariot of Sol—the sun.

ET′NA or ÆT′NA. A volcanic mountain, beneath which, according to Virgil, there is burned the giant Typhon, who breathes forth devouring flames.

ESCULA′PIUS. In mythology the god of medicine, the son of Apollo by the nymph Coronis. His worship prevailed over all Greece. In the Homeric poems Esculapius is not a divinity, but simply the "blameless physician." He is usually represented as an old man. The most characteristic emblem of Esculapius is the serpent. The name is often used as a general term for doctor.

Esculapius, Capitoline Museum, Rome.

ETE′OCLES. A king of Thebes, son of Œdipus and Jocasta. After his father's death it was agreed between him and his brother Polynices that they should reign a year each alternately. Eteocles first ascended the throne, but at the end of the year he refused to resign the crown. Thus treated, Polynices implored assistance from Adrastus, king of Argos, whose daughter he married, and who placed an army at his disposal. Eteocles marshalled his forces, and several skirmishes took place between the hostile hosts, when it was agreed on that the brothers should decide the contest by single combat. They fought with inveterate fury, and both were killed.

ETNOR′IA. A country in central Italy. The inhabitants were called Etrusci or Tusci.

EUBOCA. The largest island of the Ægæan sea.

EUCLI′DES. A famous mathematician of Alexandria, who lived B. C. 300. He wrote fifteeen books on the elements of mathematics. Euclid was so much respected that King Ptolemy became one of its pupils.

EU′MENES. A Greek officer in the army of Alexander. He was the most worthy of Alexander's generals to succeed him after his death. He conquered Paphlagonia and Cappadocia, of which he obtained the government, till the power of Antigonus obliged him to retire. Eventually, after many vicissitudes of fortune, he was put to death in prison by order of Antigonus.

MYTHOLOGICAL DICTIONARY.

EUMEN'IDES. A name given to the Furies. They sprang from the drops of blood which flowed from a wound which Cœlus received from Saturn. According to some writers they were daughters of the Earth, and sprung from the blood of Saturn. Others make them to be daughters of Acheron and Night, or Pluto and Proserpine. According to the generally received opinion they were three in number—Tisiphone, Megara, and Alecto, to which some add Nemesis. They were sometimes called Erinnys and Furiæ.

EUPHOR'BUS. A famous Trojan. He wounded Patroclus, whom Hector killed. He died by the hand of Menelaus.

EUPHRA'TES. A large river in Asia which flowed through the middle of the city of Babylon.

EURIP'IDES. A celebrated tragic poet born at Salamis. He studied eloquence under Prodicus, ethics under Socrates, and philosophy under Anaxagoras. He often retired to a solitary cave, where he wrote his tragedies. It is said that he met his death by being attacked and torn to pieces by dogs, 407 years before the Christian era, in the seventy-eighth year of his age. He is accredited with the authorship of seventy-five tragedies, of which only nineteen are extant.

EURO'PA. A daughter of Agenor, king of Phœnicia and Telaphassa. Her beauty attracted Jupiter, and to become possessed of her he assumed the shape of a handsome bull, and mingled with the herds of Agenor while Europa was gathering flowers in the meadows. She caressed the animal and mounted on his back. The god crossed the sea with her, and arrived in Crete, where he assumed his proper form, and declared his love. She became mother of Minos, Sarpedon, and Rhadamanthus.

EURYD'ICE. The wife of the poet Orpheus. As she fled from Aristæus, who was enamored with her, she was bitten by a serpent, and died of the wound. Orpheus was disconsolate at her loss, and descended to the infernal regions in search of her, and by the melody of his lyre he obtained from Pluto the restoration of Eurydice, provided he did not look behind him until he reached the earth; but his eagerness to see his wife caused him to violate the conditions, and he looked behind him, thus losing Eurydice forever.

EURYD'ICE. Wife of Amyntas, king of Macedonia, Alexander, Perdiccas, and Philip were their sons, and they had a daughter named Euryone. She conspired against Amyntas, but was prevented from killing him by Euryone.

EURYS'THENES. A son of Aristodemus, who lived in perpetual dissension with his twin brother Procles while they both sat on the Spartan throne. The descendants of Eurysthenes were called Eurysthenidæ, and those of Procles, Proclidæ.

EURYS'THEUS. A king of Argos and Mycenæ, son of Sthenelus and Nicippe. Juno hastened his birth by two months that he might come into the world before Hercules, the son of Alcmena, as the younger of the two was doomed by Jupiter to be subservient to the other. This natural right was cruelly exercised by Eurystheus, who was jealous of the fame of Hercules, and who, to destroy him, imposed upon him the most dangerous enterprises, known as the Twelve "Labors of Hercules," all of which were successfully accomplished.

EUSE'BIUS. A bishop of Cæsarea, in favor with the Emperor Constantine. He was mixed up in the theological disputes of Arius and Athanasius, and distinguished himself by writing an ecclesiastical history and other works.

EUTER'PE. One of the Muses, considered as presiding over lyric poetry, because the invention of the flute is ascribed to her. She is usually represented as a virgin crowned with flowers, having a flute in her hand, or with various instruments about her. As her name denotes, she is the inspirer of pleasure.

EUTRO'PIUS. A Latin historian in the age of Julian, the apostate. He wrote an epitome of the history of Rome from the age of Romulus to the reign of the emperor Valens.

Euterpe, from the Vatican.

F

FA'BII. A noble and powerful family at Rome. They fought with the Veientes, and all of them were slain. One of the family, of tender age, remained in Rome, and from him descended the family which afterwards became so distinguished.

FA'BIUS, MAX'IMUS RULLIA'NUS, was the first of the Fabii who obtained the name of 'Maximus." He was master of the horse, and his victory over the Samnites in that capacity nearly cost him his life. He was five times consul, twice dictator, and once censor.

FA'BIUS, Q. MAX'IMUS. A celebrated Roman who was raised to the highest offices of state. In his first consulship he obtained a victory over Liguria, and the battle of Thrasymenus caused his election to the dictatorship. In this office he opposed Hannibal, harassing him more by countermarches and ambuscades than fighting in the open field. He died at the age of 100, after being consul five times. Others of the family were of minor distinction, though their names occur in Roman history.

FABRIC'IUS, CAI'US. A distinguished Roman who in his first consulship obtained several victories over the Samnites and Lucanians. He had the most consummate knowledge of military matters, and was distinguished for the simplicity of his manners.

FALER'NUS. A fertile mountain and plain of Campania, famous for its wine. Falernian wine was held in great esteem by the Romans, and it is often alluded to by the poets.

FAME was a poetical deity, represented as having wings and blowing a trumpet. A temple was dedicated to her by the Romans.

FATE, see Nereus.

FATES, or **PARCÆ,** were the three daughters of Necessity. Their names were Clotho, who held the distaff; Lachesis, who turned the spindle; and Atropos, who cut the thread with the fatal shears.

FAU'NI. Rural deities represented as having the legs, feet, and ears of goats, and the rest of the body human. They are the same as the Greek satyrs.

FEROHER. A symbol or representation of the solar deity, seen on many of the monuments exhumed from the ruins of Nineveh and Babylon, at Persepolis, etc. Sometimes it simply appears as a winged circle; at others it consists of the demi-figure of the god, with expanded wings, and in the act of discharging an arrow from his bow; and this is the highest or most æsthetical of its various developments. A similar figure or symbol has also been found on monuments in Mexico and Central America.

Feroher, from Bonomi's Nineveh and its Palaces.

FERO'NIA, the Roman goddess of orchards, was patroness of enfranchised slaves. Some authors think Feronia is the same as Juno.

FLAC'CUS. A consul who marched against Sylla, and was assassinated.

FLAMIN'IUS, T. Q. A famous Roman who was trained in the art of war againt Hannibal. He was sent in command of the Roman troops against Philip of Macedonia, and met with great success.

FLO'RA. The goddess of flowers and gardens among the Romans. She was the same as the Chloris of the Greeks.

FORTU'NA. A powerful deity among the ancients, daughter of Oceanus according to Homer, or one of the Parcæ according to Pindar. She was the goddess of Fortune, and bestowed riches or poverty on mankind.

FOR'UM. An open space of ground where people met for the transaction of any kind of business. At Rome there were several, some used as courts and others as markets.

FRAUD, one of the evil deities, was represented as a goddess with a human face and a serpent's body, and in the end of her tail was a scorpion's sting. She lived in the river Cocytus, and nothing but her head was ever seen.

FREY'R. The Scandinavian god of fertility and peace. The patron god of Sweden and Iceland.

FREY'JA. The Scandinavian Venus. The goddess of love.

FRI'GA. The Saxon goddess of earthly enjoyments. The name Friday is derived from her. In Scandinavian mythology she is the goddess of marriage.

FRO. The Scandinavian god of tempests and winds.

FUL'VIA. An ambitious woman, wife of the tribune Clodius, afterwards of Curio, and lastly of Antony. Antony divorced her for Cleopatra. She attempted to avenge her wrongs by persuading Augustus to take up arms against Antony.

FUR'IAE. See Eumenides.

G

GALLAN'TES, madmen, from Galli (which see).

GAL'LI were priests of Cybele who used to cut their arms with knives when they sacrificed, and acted so like madmen that demented people got the name of Gallantes.

GAL'BA, Roman emperor A. D. 68–69. Succeeded by Otho.

GAN'ESA. The Indian Mercury. The god of wisdom and prudence.

GANGA. One of the three Indian river goddesses.

GA'BRIEL, in Jewish mythology is the prince of fire and thunder, and the angel of death to the favored people of God.

GALATÆ'A. A sea nymph, daughter of Nereus and Doris. She was loved by Polyphemus, the Cyclops, whom she treated with disdain, while she was in love with Acis, a shepherd of Sicily.

GAL'BA, SER'VIUS SULPI'CIUS. A Roman who rose to the greatest offices of the state, and exercised his powers with equity till he was seated on the throne, when his virtues disappeared. He was assassinated in the seventy-third year of his age.

GAL'LIA or GAUL. The country occupying what is now France, Switzerland, and northwestern Italy.

GALLIE'NUS, PUB. LICIN'IUS. A son of the emperor Valerian. He reigned conjointly with his father for seven years, and then became sole emperor, A. D. 260. In his youth he showed military ability in an expedition against the Germans and Sarmatæ, but when possessed of the purple he gave himself up to pleasure and vice. He was assassinated in his fiftieth year, A. D. 268.

GAL'LUS CORNE'LIUS. A Roman knight famous for his poetical as well as his military talents. He was greatly attached to his slave Lycoris (or Cytheris), whose beauty he extolled in his poetry.

GANYME'DES. A beautiful youth of Phrygia. He was taken to heaven by Jupiter while tending flocks on Mount Ida, and he became the cup-bearer of the gods in place of Hebe.

GEL'LIUS, AU'LUS. A Roman grammarian in the age of M. Antoninus. He wrote a work called "Noctes Atticæ," which he composed at Athens.

GERMAN'ICUS CÆ'SAR. A son of Drusus and Antonia, the niece of Augustus. He was raised to the most important position in the state, and was employed in war in Germany, where his successes obtained him a triumph. He was secretly poisoned, A. D. 19, in the thirty-fourth year of his age. He has been commended not only for his military talents but for his learning and humanity.

GE'RYON. A monster, represented by the poets as having three bodies and three heads. It was killed by Hercules.

GIGAN'TES. The sons of Cœlus and Terra, who, according to Hesiod, sprang from the blood of a wound inflicted on Cœlus by his son Saturn. They are represented as huge giants, with strength in accordance with their size.

GLAU'CUS. 1. A son of Hippolochus, the son of Bellerophon. He aided Priam in the Trojan war, and was noted for his folly in exchanging his golden armor with Diomedes for an iron one. 2. A fisherman of Bœotia. He observed that the fishes which he caught and laid on the grass became invigorated and leaped into the sea. He tasted the grass, and suddenly felt a desire to live in the sea. He was made a sea deity by Oceanus and Tethys. 3. A son of Minos the Second and Pasiphae, who was smothered in a cask of honey. The soothsayer Polyidus on being commanded by Minos to find his son, discovered him and by rubbing his body with a certain herb restored him to life.

GLY'CON An Athenian sculptor, famous for his statue of Hercules.

GOLDEN FLEECE, THE, was a ram's hide, sometimes described as white, and at other times as purple and golden. It was given to Phryxus, who carried it to Colchis, where King Æta entertained Phryxus, and the hide was hung up in the grove of Mars. Jason and forty-nine companions fetched back the golden fleece.

GORDIA'NUS, M. ANTO'NIUS AFRICA'NUS. Son of Metius Marcellus. He applied himself to poetry, and composed a poem in thirty books. He was sent as proconsul to Africa, and subsequently, when he had attained his eightieth year, he was proclaimed emperor. He strangled himself at Carthage A. D. 236, and was deeply lamented by the army and the people.

GORDIA'NUS, M. ANTO'NIUS AFRICA'NUS, son of Gordianus, was made prefect of Rome, and afterwards consul by Alexander Severus. He was elected emperor in conjunction with his father. He was killed in a battle fought with Maximinus in Mauritania.

GORDIA'NUS, M. ANTO'NIUS PI'US, was grandson of the first Gordian. He was proclaimed emperor in the sixteenth year of his age. He married the daughter of Misetheus, who was distinguished by his virtues, and to whom Gordian entrusted many of the chief offices of the state. Gordian conquered Sapor, king of Persia, and took many cities from him. He was assassinated A. D. 244.

GOR'DIUS. A Phrygian who, from the position of a peasant, was raised to the throne consequent on a prediction of the oracle. The knot which tied the yoke to the draught-tree of his chariot was made so cunningly that the ends of the cord could not be seen, and a report arose that the empire of Asia was promised by the oracle to him who should untie the Gordian knot. Alexander cut the knot with his sword.

GOR'GONES (the Gorgons). Three sisters, daughters of Phorcys and Ceto, whose names were Stheno, Euryale, and Medusa. They possessed the power of turning into stone those on whom they looked. Perseus attacked them and cut off Medusa's head, which he gave to Minerva, who placed it on her ægis, which turned into stone those who fixed their eyes on it.

GRAC'CHUS, T. SEMPRONIUS, was twice consul and once

censor. He married Cornelia, of the family of the Scipios, a woman of piety and learning. Their children, Tiberius and Caius, rendered themselves famous for their obstinate attachment to the interests of the populace, which at last proved fatal to them. The Gracchi stand out conspicuously in Roman annals.

GRACES, THE, were the attendants of Venus. Their names were, Aglaia, so called from her beauty and goodness; Thalia, from her perpetual freshness; and Euphrosyne, from her cheerfulness. They are generally depicted as three cheerful maidens with hands joined, and either nude, or only wearing transparent robes,—the idea being that kindnesses, as personified by the Graces, should be done with sincerity and candor and without disguise. They were supposed to teach the duties of gratitude and friendship, and they promoted love and harmony among mankind.

GYMNA'SIUM. A place among the Greeks where all the public exercises were performed, and where not only dancers and wrestlers exhibited, but where poets and philosophers epeated their compositions.

H

HA'DES. See Ades.

HAD'NAN'US, P. ÆLIUS, usually called Hadnan, Roman emperor A. D. 117–138. Succeeded Trajan.

HALICARNAS'SUS. A maritime city in Asia Minor, where a mausoleum, one of the seven wonders of the world, was erected. It is celebrated as being the birthplace of Herodotus, Dionysius, and Heraclitus.

HAMADRY'ADES. Nymphs who lived in the country and presided over trees.

HAMIL'CAR. A famous Carthaginian, father of Hannibal. He was engaged in Sicily during the first Punic war. He used to say of his three sons that he kept three lions to devour the Roman power.

HAN'NIBAL. A celebrated Carthaginian general, son of Hamilcar. While a child he took a solemn oath never to be at peace with Rome. His passage of the Alps with a great army was achieved by softening the rocks with fire and vinegar, so that even his armed elephants descended the mountains without difficulty. He defeated the Romans in the great battle of Cannæ, but was subsequently conquered by Scipio at Zama. He died by poison taken from a ring in which he kept it concealed. This occurred in his seventieth year, about 182 years B. C.

HARMO'DIUS. A friend of Aristogiton who assisted in delivering his country from the tyranny of the Pisistratidæ.

HARPY. A fabulous winged monster, ravenous and filthy, having the face of a woman and the body of a bird, with its feet and fingers armed with sharp claws, and the face pale with hunger. The harpies were three in number, Aello, Ocypete, and Celeno. In heraldry the harpy is represented as a vulture with the head and breast of a woman.

Harpy, from an antique gem.

HAS'DRUBAL. A son of Hamilcar, and brother of Hannibal. He crossed the Alps and entered Italy, where he was defeated by the consuls, M. Livius Salinator and Claudius Nero. He was killed in the battle B. C. 207, and his head was sent to Hannibal.

HE'BE. A daughter of Jupiter and Juno. She was made cup-bearer to the gods, but was dismissed from the office by Jupiter, because she fell down in a clumsy posture as she was pouring out nectar at a festival, and Ganymedes succeeded her as cup-bearer. She had the power of restoring the aged to the bloom of youth and beauty. She was called Juventes by the Romans. Statues of her are rare, and she is only to be recognized by the cup in which she presented the nectar. Sometimes she holds in the right hand a vase from which the cup was filled.

Hebe.

"Wreathed smiles,
Such as hang on Hebe's cheek,
And love to live in dimple sweet."
MILTON.

HEC'ATE. A daughter of Perses and Asteria. She was

called Luna in heaven, Diana on earth, and Hecate or Proserpine in hell.

HEC'TOR, son of King Priam and Hecuba, was the most valiant of all the Trojan chiefs who fought against the Greeks. He married Andromache, daughter of Eetion, Astyanax being their son. Hector was made chief of the Trojan forces when Troy was besieged by the Greeks, and it is said that thirty-one of the most valiant Greek chiefs were killed by him, but when he met Achilles he fled. Achilles pursued him, and Hector was killed, and his body dragged in triumph at the chariot wheels of the conqueror.

HEC'UBA, daughter of Dymas, a Phrygian prince, or, according to some, of Cisseus, a Thracian king, was the second wife of Priam, king of Troy. When her son Paris was born, she exposed him on Mount Ida, hoping he would perish, as the soothsayers had predicted that he would be the ruin of his country. In the Trojan war she saw most of her children perish. After enduring many misfortunes, she threw herself into the sea, and was drowned.

HEL'ENA. One of the most beautiful women in the age in which she lived. Her beauty was so universally admired, even in her infancy, that Theseus, with his friend Pirithous, carried her away when she was ten years of age and concealed her with his mother, but she was recovered by Castor and Pollux, and restored to her native country. She married Menelaus, son of Atreus, but when Paris visited Menelaus he persuaded her to fly with him to Troy B. C. 1198. On this, Menelaus sent ambassadors to the court of Priam to demand her restitution, but in vain, and the result was the Trojan war. When Troy was taken she returned to Menelaus, and after his death she retired to Rhodes, where she was strangled by order of Polyxo, who reigned there. Her beauty and misfortunes have been a theme for the poets in all ages; one of them thus speaks of her:—

> "Possess'd of all those glowing charms,
> That fir'd the Trojan boy,
> And kindled love with war's alarms
> Around the walls of Troy."

He′liades were the daughters of Sol, and the sisters of Phaeton, at whose death they were so sad that they stood mourning till they became metamorphosed into poplar trees, and their tears were turned into amber.

Hel′icon. A mountain of Bœotia on the borders of Phocis. It was sacred to the Muses, who had a temple there. The fountain Hippocrene flowed from this mountain.

Heliogab′alus, M. Aure′lius Antoni′nus. A Roman emperor who had been priest to a divinity in Phœnicia. Under his sway Rome became the scene of cruelty and vice. He raised his horse to the honors of consulship, and indulged in a number of absurdities which rendered him odious to his subjects. His head was cut off by his soldiers A. D. 222.

Hel′le. A daughter of Athamas and Nephele. She fled from her father's house to avoid the oppression of her mother-in-law Ino. According to some accounts, she was carried through the air on a golden ram, when, becoming giddy, she fell into the sea, which received from her the name Hellespont.

Hellespon′tus. A narrow strait between Europe and Asia, which received its name from Helle, who is said to have been drowned in it. It is celebrated as being the scene of the love and death of Leander.

Hephaes′tus, called Vulcanus by the Romans, the god of fire. He was the son of Zeus (Jupiter) and Hera (Juno).

Her′cules. A celebrated hero who, after death, was ranked among the gods. According to the ancients there were many persons of the same name, but the son of Jupiter and Alcmena, generally called the Theban, is the most celebrated. The birth of Hercules was attended with many miraculous events. Before he was eight months old Juno sent two snakes to devour him, which he seized, and crushed them to death. He achieved a series of enterprises known as the "Twelve

Hercules slaying the Hydra—from sculpture at Florence.

Labors of Hercules." These comprised the slaughter of the Nemæan lion, the destruction of the Lernæan hydra, the catching of a stag having golden horns and remarkable for his swiftness, the seizing alive a wild boar which committed great ravages, the cleansing of the stables of Augeas, the killing of the carnivorous birds near Lake Stymphalis, the taking captive a prodigious wild bull, the obtaining the mares of Diomedes which fed on human flesh, the getting possession of the girdle of the queen of the Amazons, the destruction of the monster Geryon, the obtaining the apples from the garden of the Hesperides, and the bringing to the earth the three-headed dog Cerberus. Besides these labors he aided the gods in their wars with the giants, and performed numerous difficult feats. He was conducted by Mercury to Omphale, queen of Lydia, whom he married, and whom he permitted to dress in his armor while he was sitting to spin with her female servants. He delivered Dejanira from the Centaur Nessus, whom he killed. The Centaur, as he expired, gave Dejanira a mystic tunic, which, in a jealous paroxysm, she gave to Hercules to put on, which he had no sooner done than he was seized with a desperate distemper which was incurable. He erected a burning pile on Mount Æta, on which he cast himself. Jupiter surrounded the burning pile with smoke, in the midst of which Hercules, after his mortal parts were consumed, was carried to heaven in a chariot drawn by four horses.

HERACLI'TUS. A celebrated Greek philosopher of Ephesus, who lived about 500 years before the Christian era. He received the appellation of the Obscure Philosopher and the Mourner, from his custom of weeping at the follies and frailties of human life.

HERCULA'NEUM. A town of Campania swallowed up by an earthquake, produced by an eruption of Mount Vesuvius A. D. 79.

HERMI'ONE. A daughter of Menelaus and Helen. She was privately promised in marriage to Orestes, the son of Agamemnon, but her father, ignorant of the engagement, gave her hand to Pyrrhus, the son of Achilles, whose services he had experienced in the Trojan war.

HERMES. The name given to Mercury by the Greeks. In Greek antiquity a statue composed of a head, usually that of the god Hermes, placed on a quadrangular pillar, the height of which corresponded to the stature of the human body. The Athenian houses had one of these statues placed at the door, and sometimes also in the peristyle. The hermæ were held in great reverence. They were likewise placed in front of temples, near to tombs, in the gymnasia, libraries, porticos, and public places, at the corners of streets, on high-roads as sign-posts with distances inscribed upon them, and on the boundaries of lands and states, and at the gates of cities.

Hermes or Mercury.

HERMIN'IUS. A valiant Roman who defended the bridge with Cocles against the army of Porsenna. Lord Macaulay, in his noble poem "Horatius," alludes to him as one of the "dauntless three" who defended the bridge against the host of Porsenna:—

"And out spake strong Herminius,
  Of Titian blood was he,
I will abide on thy left side,
  And keep the bridge with thee."

HERMIP'PUS. A freedman, disciple of Philo, in the reign of Adrian, by whom he was greatly esteemed. He wrote five books on dreams.

HERMOC'RATES. A general of Syracuse, who was sent against the Athenians. His lenity toward the Athenian prisoners was regarded with suspicion. He was banished from Sicily, and was murdered on his attempt to return to his country.

HERMODO'RUS. A philosopher of Ephesus who is said to have assisted, as interpreter, the Roman decemvirs in the composition of the ten tables of laws which had been collected in Greece.

HE'RO. A beautiful girl of Sestos greatly beloved by Leander, a youth of Abydos. The lovers were greatly attached to each other, and often in the night Leander swam across the Hellespont to Hero in Sestos, till on one tempestuous night he was drowned, and Hero in despair threw herself into the sea and perished.

HER'ODES, surnamed the Great, followed the fortunes of Brutus and Cassius, and afterwards those of Antony. He was made king of Judæa by the aid of Antony, and after the battle of Actium he was continued in power by submission to and flattery of Augustus. He rendered himself odious by his cruelty, and as he knew his death would be a cause for rejoicing, he ordered a number of the most illustrious of his subjects to be confined and murdered directly he expired, that there might appear to be grief and shedding of tears for his own death. Herod died in the seventieth year of his age, after a reign of 40 years.

HEROD'OTUS. A celebrated historian of Halicarnassus. He ranks among historians as Homer does among the poets and Demosthenes among the orators. His great work is a history of the wars of the Persians against the Greeks, from the age of Cyrus to the battle of Mycale in the reign of Xerxes; besides which it gives an account of many celebrated nations. A life of Homer is attributed to his pen, though by some the authorship is doubted. He was born B. C. 484.

HESI'ODUS. A celebrated poet, born at Ascra in Bœotia. He lived in the age of Homer, and obtained a poetical prize in competition with him, according to Varro and Plutarch. Quintilian, Philostratus, and others, maintain that Hesiod lived before the age of Homer. Hesiod, without possessing the sublimity of Homer, is admired for the elegance of his diction.

HESI'ONE. A daughter of Laodemon, king of Troy. It was her fate to be exposed to a sea monster, to whom the Trojans presented yearly a young girl to appease the resentment of Apollo and Neptune, whom Laodemon had offended. Hercules undertook to rescue her, and attacking the monster just as he was about to devour her, killed him with his club.

HESPER'IDES. Three Nymphs, daughters of Hesperus. Apollodorus mentions four, Ægle, Erythia, Vesta and Arethusa. They were appointed to guard the golden apples which Juno gave to Jupiter on the day of their marriage. The place where the Hesperides lived was a celebrated garden, abounding with delicious fruit, and was guarded by a dragon which never slept. It was one of the labors of Hercules to procure some of the golden apples, which he succeeded in doing after slaying the dragon.

HESPERUS, the evening star.

HIER'ON. A tyrant of Sicily, who succeeded to the throne when he was fifteen years old. He rendered himself odious by his cruelty and oppression.

HIERON'YMUS. A Christian writer, commonly called St. Jerome. He was distinguished for his zeal against heretics. He wrote commentaries on the prophets, St. Matthew's Gospel, etc. He died A. D. 420, in his eightieth year.

HIP'PIAS, the sophist, a Greek philosopher, contemporary with Socrates.

HIPPAR'CHUS. A son of Pisistratus, who succeeded his father, as tyrant of Athens, with his brother Hippias. He patronized some of the learned men of his age, and distinguished himself for his love of literature.

HIPPOC'RATES. A celebrated physician of Cos. He delivered Athens from a dreadful pestilence in the beginning of the Peloponnesian war, for which he was rewarded with a golden crown. He died in his ninety-ninth year, B. C. 361.

HIPPOC'RENE. A fountain of Bœotia, near Mount Helicon, sacred to the Muses. It rose from the ground when struck by the feet of the horse Pegasus.

HIPPOCRAM'PUS. The name of Neptune's (Poseidon) favorite horse.

HIPPOCRE'NIDES, a name of the Muses, from the fountain of Hippocrene (the horse fountain), which was formed by a kick of the winged horse Pegasus.

HIPPODAMI'A. A daughter of Œnomaus, king of Pisa, who married Pelops, son of Tantalus. Her father would marry her only to some one who should conquer him in a chariot race. Her beauty was great, and many were competitors for her hand, though the conditions involved death in case of defeat in the race. After thirteen suitors had been defeated, Pelops entered the lists, and by bribing the charioteer of Œnomaus, obtained the victory and married Hippodamia.

Hippol'yte, queen of the Amazons, daughter of Mars. Her father gave her a famous girdle, which Hercules was required to procure (see Hercules). She was conquered by Hercules, and given by him in marriage to Theseus.

Hippol'ytus. Son of Theseus and Hippolyte. His stepmother Phædra fell in love with him. He fled to the seashore, where, his horses taking fright and rushing among the rocks, his chariot was broken to pieces, and he was killed. According to some accounts he was restored to life by Diana (Artemis).

Hippo'nax. A Greek poet born at Ephesus, 540 years before the Christian era. He cultivated satirical poetry, which was marked by its beauty and vigor.

Ho'mer. A celebrated Greek poet, the most ancient of all the profane writers. The age in which he lived is not known, though some suppose it to be about 168 years after the Trojan war. Uncertainty prevails, also, as to the place of his nativity, seven cities claiming to be thus honored. These are Smyrna, Chios, Colophon, Salamis, Rhodes, Argos, and Athenæ. In his two famous poems, the Iliad and Odyssey, he has displayed the most consummate knowledge of human nature, and rendered himself immortal by the sublimity and elegance of his poetry. In the Iliad he gives a narrative of the siege of Troy, and the Odyssey deals with the wanderings of Ulysses after the fall of the city. Byron, in "The Bride of Abydos," calls him

"The blind old man of Scio's rocky isle,"

thus assuming Chios to be his birthplace, Scio being the modern name of the place. Dryden, in his well-known lines commencing

"Three poets in three distant ages born,"

ranks him with Virgil and Milton, giving Homer the palm for "loftiness of thought." One of the old poets thus alludes to his verse:—

> "Read Homer once, and you can read no more,
> For all books else appear so mean and poor;
> Verse will seem prose; but still persist to read,
> And Homer will be all the books you need."

Hono′rius. An emperor of the Western Empire of Rome, who succeeded his father, Theodosius the Great. He conquered his enemies by the ability of his generals, and suffered his people to be governed by ministers who took advantage of his indolence and indifference. He died A. D. 423.

Hora′tii. Three brave Romans, born at the same time, who fought against the three Curiatii about 667 years before Christ. At the beginning of the fight two of the Horatii were killed, and the surviving one pretended to fly, thus separating his antagonists as they pursued him, and then, attacking them singly, he slew them all.

Hora′tius, Q. Flac′cus. A celebrated poet born at Venusia. His rising talents obtained the attention of Virgil and Varius, who recommended him to the care of Mæcenas and Augustus, the celebrated patrons of literature. Under this fostering patronage Horace gave himself up to indolence and pleasure. He was warm in his friendships, and if he at any time gave offence, he was ready to make any concession to effect a reconciliation. In his satires and epistles he displays much wit and satirical humor. He died in his fifty-seventh year, B. C. 8.

Horten′sius, Q. A celebrated orator who began to distinguish himself in the Roman Forum when he was nineteen years old. Cicero speaks eulogistically of his oratorical powers, and of his retentive memory. Quintilian alludes to his orations in terms of high commendation.

Hyacin′thus. A son of Amyclas and Diomede, greatly beloved by Apollo and Zephyrus. He was accidentally killed by Apollo, who changed his blood into a flower which bore his name.

Hy′ades, a name given to the nymphs.

Hy′bla. A mountain in Sicily, famous for the odoriferous herbs which grew on it. It was famous for its honey.

Hy′dra. A celebrated monster which infested the neighborhood of Lake Lerna in Peloponnesus. It was one of the labors of Hercules to destroy the monster, which he effected with the aid of Iolas.

HYGEIA. The goddess of health, daughter of Esculapius. She is represented as a blooming maid with a bowl in one hand and grasping a serpant with the other. She was held in great veneration among the ancients.

HYMENÆ'US or HY'MEN, the god of marriage among the Greeks, was the son of Bacchus and Venus, or according to some, of Apollo and one of the Muses. He was represented as a handsome youth, holding in his hand a burning torch.

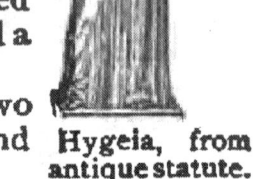

Hygeia, from antique statute.

HYMET'TUS. A mountain of Attica, about two miles from Athens, famous for its bees and honey.

HYPERI'ON. A son of Cœlus and Terra, who married Thea. Aurora was their daughter. Hyperion is ofted used by the poets to signify the sun: as, for instance, by Shakspeare in "Titus Andronicus" (act v. sc. 2)—

"Even from Hyperion's rising in the east,
Until his very downfall in the sea."

HYPERMNES'TRA. One of the Danaides, who were the fifty daughters of Danaus. She was ordered by her father to murder her husband Lynceus on the night of their marriage, which she refused to do. Danaus wished to punish her for her disobedience, but afterwards forgave her, and left his kingdom at his death to Lynceus.

HYPSIP'YLE. A queen of Lemnos, daughter of Thoas. During her reign, Venus, whose altars had been slighted, punished the Lemnian women by causing their husbands' affections to be estranged from them. This enraged the women, and they put to death their male relations, except in the case of Hypsipyle, who spared her father Thoas.

I

IAC'CHUS. A name of Bacchus.

IC'ARUS. A son of Daedalus, who, with his father, took a winged flight from Crete to escape the anger of Minos. 's flight was too high, and thus the sun melted the wax which cemented his wings, and he fell into the sea and was drowned.

IDOM'ENEUS succeeded his father Deucalion on the throne of Crete, and accompanied the Greeks to the Trojan war during which he rendered himself famous for his valor. On his voyage home, being caught in a great tempest, he vowed to Neptune that if he escaped he would make an offering to the god of the first living creature he saw on his arrival at the Cretan shore. He escaped the storm, and the first to meet him on his landing was his son. He performed his vow, and became so odious to his subjects that he had to leave his dominions.

IGNA'TIUS. A bishop of Antioch torn to pieces by lions in the amphitheatre at Rome A. D. 107. His works consisted of letters to the Ephesians, Romans, etc. He zealously supported the doctrine of the divinity of Christ.

I'LUS, fourth king of Troy, was son of Tros by Callirrhoe. He married Eurydic the daughter of Adrastus. He embellished the city of Ilium, called also Troy from his father Tros.

INDRA. A Hindoo deity originally representing the sky or heavens, and worshipped as the supreme god, though he afterwards assumed a subordinate place in the Indian mythology. He is represented in various ways in painting and sculpture, especially with four arms and hands, and riding on an elephant. When painted he is covered with eyes. In the oldest Vedic hymns the character of Indra is that of a mighty ruler of the bright firmament, at once beneficent, as giving rain and shade, and awful and powerful, as in the storm. He sends refreshing rain, and wields the thunderbolt, at the crash of which heaven and earth quake with terror.

Indra.

I'NO. A daughter of Cadmus and Harmonia, who nursed Bacchus. She married Athamus, king of Thebes, after he had divorced Nephele. Ino had two children, who could not ascend the throne while Phryxus and Helle were alive.

Ino therefore persecuted them to such a degree that they determined to escape. They did so on a ram, whose hide became the Golden Fleece (see Phryxes and Helle). Ino destroyed herself, and was changed by Neptune (Poseidon) into a sea-goddess.

INO'A were festivals in memory of Ino.

I'O, a daughter of Inachus, was a priestess of Juno (Hera) at Argos. Jupiter (Zeus) changed her into a beautiful heifer, and eventually restored her to her own form. She was greatly persecuted by Juno. She married Telegonus, king of Egypt, or Osiris according to others, and treated her subjects with such kindness that after death she received divine honors, and was worshipped under the name of Isis.

I'OLAS or IOLA'US. A son of Iphiclus, king of Thessaly, who assisted Hercules in conquering the Hydra; he burnt with a hot iron the place where the monsters' heads had been cut off to prevent their re-growth.

IONI'A. A district on the western coast of Asia Minor; principal cities were Miletus, Ephesus, Chios, Phocæa.

IPH'ICLUS. A son of Amphitryon and Alcmena, twin brother of Hercules. As the children were carried together, Juno (Hera), jealous of Hercules, sent two large serpents to destroy him. At the sight of the snakes Iphiclus showed great alarm, but Hercules seized them, one in each hand, and squeezed them to death.

IPHIC'RATES. A celebrated general of Athens, who, though son of a shoemaker, rose to the highest office in the state. He made war against the Thracians, and assisted the Persian king against Egypt. Died 348 B. C.

IPHIGENI'A. A daughter of Agamemnon and Clytemnestra. When the Greeks, going to the Trojan war, were detained at Aulis by contrary winds, they were informed by a soothsayer that to appease the gods they must sacrifice Iphigenia to Diana (Artemis). As the fatal knife was about to be plunged into her, Iphigenia suddenly disappeared, and a goat of great beauty was found in the place where she had stood ready for the sacrifice.

˷US. A son of Eurytus, king of Œchalia. When his ˷r had promised his daughter Iole to any one who excel him or his sons in drawing the bow, Hercules accepted the challenge and was victorious. Eurytus, however, refused to fulfill the compact by giving his daughter to the conquerer. Afterwards some oxen were stolen from Eurytus, and Iphitus was sent in quest of them. In his search he met Hercules, who aided him in seeking the lost animals, but on recollecting the faithlessness of Eurytus he killed Iphitus.

IRENÆ'US. A native of Greece, disciple of Polycarp, and bishop of Lyons. He wrote on different subjects, and suffered martyrdom A. D. 202.

I'RIS. One of the Oceanides, messenger of the gods, and more particularly of Juno (Hera). Her office was to cut the thread which seemed to detain the soul of those who were expiring. She is the same as the rainbow.

I'SIS. One of the chief deities in the Egyptian mythology. She was regarded as the sister or sister-wife of Osiris, and the mother of Horus. She was worshipped by the Egyptians as the being who had first civilized them, and taught them agriculture and other necessary arts of life. Among the higher and more phylosophical theologians she was made the symbol of pantheistic divinity. By the people she was worshipped as the goddess of fecundity. The cow was sacred to her. She is represented variously, though most usually as a woman with the horns of a cow, between which is a globe supporting a throne, and sometimes with the lotus on her head and the sistrum in her hand.

Isis.

ISOC'RATES. A celebrated orator, son of a musical instrument maker at Athens. He opened a school of eloquence at Athens, where he was distinguished for the number, character and fame of his pupils. He was intimate with Philip of Macedon, but the aspiring ambition of Philip displeased Isocrates, and the defeat of the Athenians at Chæronea had such an effect on him that he did not long survive it. He died after being four days without taking any ailment, in his ninety-ninth year, about 338 years before Christ. Milton, in one of his sonnets, speaks of him as " that old man eloquent."

I'TYS. A son of Tereus, king of Thrace, and Procne, daughter of Pandion, king of Athens. He was killed by his mother when he was six years old, and served up to his father to be eaten by him. He was changed into a pheasant, his mother into a swallow, and his father into an owl.

IXI'ON. King of Thessaly, son of Phlegias, or, according to Hyginus, of Leontes, or, according to Diodorus, of Antion and Perimela. Jupiter (Zeus) carried him to heaven and placed him at the table of the gods, where he became enamored with Juno (Hera), which so incensed Jupiter that he banished him from heaven, and ordered Mercury (Hermes) to tie him to a wheel in hell which continually whirled round, keeping Ixion in perpetual torture.

J

J'ANI was a place in Rome where there were three statues of Janus, and it was a meeting-place for usurers and creditors.

JA'NITOR. A title of Janus, from the gates before the doors of private houses being called Januæ.

JA'NUS. An ancient king who reigned in Italy. He was a native of Thessaly, and, according to some writers, a son of Apollo. He built a town which he called Janiculum. Some authors make him to have been son of Cœlus and Hecate. He is represented with two faces, because he was acquainted with the past and future. His temple was always open in time of war, and was shut when peace existed.

JA'SON. A celebrated hero, son of Æson and Alcimedes. His education was entrusted to the Centaur Chiron. The greatest feat recorded of him is his voyage in the Argo to Colchis to obtain the Golden Fleece, which, aided by Juno (Hera), he succeeded in doing. Medea, daughter of Ætes, king of Colchis, fell in love with Jason. She was a powerful magician, and on Jason having vowed eternal fidelity to her, she gave him charms to protect him from danger. After securing the Fleece, Jason set sail from the country with his wife Medea. After some years he became enamored with Glauce, daughter of Creon, king of Corinth, whom he married, having divorced Medea. This cruel act was revenged by Medea, who destroyed her children in the presence of their father. Jason is said to have been killed by a beam which fell on his head as he was reposing by the side of the ship which had borne him to Colchis.

JOCAS'TA. A daughter of Menœceus, who married Laius, king of Thebes, Œdipus being their son. She afterwards married Œdipus without knowing who he was, and on the discovery she hanged herself. By some mythologists she is called Epicasta.

JOSE'PHUS, FLA'VIUS. A celebrated Jew, born in Jerusalem, who singalized himself in a siege conducted by Vespasian and Titus in a small town in Judæa. He was present at the siege of Jerusalem by Titus, and received all the sacred books which it contained from the conqueror's hands. He wrote a history of the wars of the Jews in Syriac, and afterwards translated it into Greek. He also wrote a work, which he divided into twenty books, on Jewish antiquities. He died A. D. 93, in his fifty-sixth year.

JOVIA'NUS, FLA'VIUS CLAU'DIUS. A native of Pannonia, elected emperor of Rome by the soldiers after the death of Julian. He refused at first, but on being assured that his subjects were favorably disposed towards Christianity he accepted the crown. He died about seven months after assuming the supreme power, being found in bed suffocated by the vapors of charcoal which had been lighted in his room, A. D. 364.

JU'BA. 1. A king of Numidia and Mauritania, son of Hiempsal, who favored the cause of Pompey against Julius Cæsar. He defeated Curio, whom Cæsar had sent to Africa, and after the battle of Pharsalia he joined his forces to those of Scipio. He was conquered in the battle at Thapsus, and killed himself. His kingdom became a Roman province, of which Sallust, the great historian, was the first governor. 2. The second of that name was led captive to Rome to give lustre to the triumph of

Cæsar. He wrote a history of Rome which was often commended and quoted by the ancients.

JUGUR'THA. A distinguished Numidian, a grandson of King Masinissa, who went with a body of troops to the assistance of Scipio who was besieging Numantia. Jugurtha endeared himself to the Roman general by his bravery and activity. His uncle Micipsa appointed him successor to the throne, with his two sons Adherbal and Hiempsal, the latter of whom was slain by Jugurtha, and the former had to fly to Rome for safety. Cæcilius Metellus was sent against Jugurtha, who was betrayed and delivered into the hands of the Romans. He died in prison, B. C. 106.

JU'LIA. 1. A daughter of Julius Cæsar and Cornelia, famous for her virtues and personal charms. She was obliged by her father to divorce herself from her first husband to marry Pompey the Great, with the object of cementing the friendship between him and her father. She died 54 years B. C. 2. Daughter of Augustus, remarkable for her beauty, genius, and vices. Her father gave her in marriage to Marcellus, after whose death she united herself to Agrippa, and again becoming a widow she married Tiberius. Her conduct now became so unseemly that the was banished to a small island on the coast of Campania, where she was starved to death. 3. A daughter of Germanicus and Agrippina, born at Lesbos, A. D. 17. She married M. Vinucius, a senator, when she was sixteen years old. She was banished on suspicion of conspiracy by her brother Caligula. She was notorious for her licentious conduct, and was put to death when she was about twenty-four years of age.

JULIA'NUS F. CLAUDIUS, Roman Emperor, A. D. 361-363. A son of Julius Constantius, the brother of Constantine the Great, born in Constantinople. The massacre which attended the elevation of the sons of Constantine to the throne nearly proved fatal to Julian and his brother Gallus. The two brothers were privately educated and taught the doctrines of the Christian religion—which afterwards Julian disavowed, and in consequence of this term "Apostate" is generally affixed to his name.

He died, A. D. 363, in his thirty-second year. His last moments were spent in a conversation with a philosopher about the immortality of his soul. Julian's character has been admired by some writers, but generally he is censured for his apostasy.

Ju′no (Hera in Greek). A celebrated deity among the ancients, daughter of Saturn and Ops. Jupiter married her, and the nuptials were celebrated wtth the greatest solemnity in the presence of all the gods. By her marriage with Jupiter (Zeus), Juno became the queen of all the gods, and mistress of heaven and earth. She presided over marriage, and patronized those of her sex who were distinguished for virtuous conduct. Paris gave her great offence by giving the golden apple, as an award to beauty, to Venus instead of herself.

Juno, from an Antique statue.

Jupiter. The supreme deity among the Latin races in Italy, the equivalent of the Greek Zeus. He received from the Romans, whose tutelary deity he was, the titles of Optimus Maximus (Best Greatest). As the deity presiding over the sky he was considered as the originator of all atmospheric changes. He was regarded as supreme in human affairs; he foresaw and directed the future, and sacrifices were offered up to him at the beginning of every undertaking in order to propitiate his favors. He was likewise believed to be the guardian of property, whether of the state or of individuals. White, the color of the light of day, was sacred to him; hence, white animals were offered up in sacrifice to him, his priests wore white caps, his chariot was represented as drawn by four white horses, and the consuls were dressed in white upon the occasion of their sacrificing to him when they entered upon office. He is often represented with

Jupiter, from an antique statue.

thunderbolts in his hand, and the eagle, his favorite bird, is generally placed by the side of his throne. Jupiter was educated in a cave on Mount Ida, in Crete, and fed with the milk of the goat Amalthæa. While he was very young he made war on the Titans, whom he conquered. The beginning of his reign in the supernal region was interrupted by the rebellion of the giants who were sons of the Earth, and who were desirous of revenging the death of the Titans, but by the aid of Hercules, Jupiter overpowered them. Jupiter married Metis, Themis, Ceres, Euronyme, Mnemosyne, Latona, and Juno. His worship was universal; he was the Ammon of the Africans, the Belus of Babylon, and the Osiris of Egypt.

JUSTI'NIANUS, Emperor of Constantinople, A. D. 527–565. He was educated a Christian, but turned heretic late in life. His greatest work was the codification of laws. It has come down to us as the *Codex Justinianeus*.

JUVENA'LIS, D. JU'NIUS. A poet born at Aquinum in Italy. He came to Rome at an early age, where he applied himself to the writing of satires, some of which are extant. He died in the reign of Trojan, A. D. 128. His writings are distinguished by a lively style, but abound with ill humor.

JUVEN'TAS   See Hebe.

K

KALI. A Hindoo goddess, after whom Calcutta is named.

KA'LOC. One of the chiefs of the ancient Mexican gods.

KAM'A. The Hindoo god of Love.

KEB'LA. The point of the compass which worshippers look to during their invocations. Thus the Sol or Sun worshippers turn to the east, where the sun rises, and the Mohammedans turn toward Mecca.

KE'DERLI, in Mohammedan mythology, is a god corresponding to the English St. George, and is still invoked by the Turks when they go to war.

KI'UN. The ancient Egyptian Venus.

KNEPH. An Egyptian god, having a ram's head and a man's body.

KRISH'NA. In Hindoo mythology, the black or dark one. The eighth incarnation of the god Vishnu, formed from one of two hairs plucked by him from his head in order to revenge the wrongs inflicted on Brahma by Kansa, the demon king, the revenger of wrongs; also called the Indian Apollo.

KRO'DO. The Saxon Saturn.

KU'MA'RA. The war-god of the Hindoos.

KU'VERA. The Hindoo god of riches

Krishna.

L

LA'BE. The Arabian Circe, who had unlimited power of metamorphosis.

LABE'RIUS, J. DEC'IMUS. A Roman knight famous for his skill in writing pantomimes. Cæsar made him appear on the stage in one of his plays, which he resented by throwing out aspersions on Cæsar during the performance, and by warning the audience against tyrany; died 43 B.C.

LACH'ESIS. One of the Parcæ, or Fates. She presided over futurity, and was represented as spinning the thread of life, or, according to some, as holding the spindle.

LAD'ON. The dragon who guarded the apples of Hesperides; was slain by Hercules.

LAER'TES. A king of Ithaca who married Anticlea, daughter of Autolycus. Ulysses was their son, and succeeded him on the throne, Laertes retiring to the country, and devoting his time to gardening, in which employment he was found by Ulysses on his return from the Trojan war, after twenty years' absence.

LÆ'LAPS. One of Diana's hunting dogs, which, while pursuing a wild boar, was petrified. Also the name of one of Actæon's hounds.

LA'GUS. A Macedonian of mean extraction who married Arsinoe, daughter of Meleager. On the birth of a child it was exposed in the woods by Lagus, but an eagle preserved its life by feeding and sheltering it with her wings.

The infant was afterwards known as King Ptolemy the First of Egypt.

LA'IS. A woman of immoral character, daughter of Timandra and Alcibiades. Diogenes, the Cynic, was one of her admirers, and gained her heart. She went to Thessaly, where the women, jealous of her charms, assassinated her.

LAOC'OON. A priest of Apollo who in the Trojan war was opposed to the admission of the wooden horse to the city. For this, as a punishment, two enormous serpents were sent to attack him, which they did, while, accompanied by his two sons, he was offering a sacrifice to Neptune (Poseidon). The serpents coiled round him and his sons, and crushed them to death. Lord Byron ("Childe Harold," canto 4) thus alludes to the Laocoon group in marble in the Vatican:—

The group of the Laocoon.

> "Or, turning to the Vatican, go see
> Laocoon's torture, dignifying pain-
> A father's love and mortal's agony
> With an immortal's patience blending."

LAODICE'A. The name of six different Greek colonies in Asia.

LAOM'EDON. Son of Ilus, and king of Troy. He married Strymo, called by some Placia or Leucippe. Podarces, afterwards known as Priam, was their son. Laomedon built the walls of Troy, in which he was assisted by Apollo and Neptune (Poseidon).

LAP'ITHES. A son of Apollo and Stilbe. He married Orsinome, Phorbas and Periphas being their children, to whose numerous descendants was given the name Lapithæ, a number of whom attended the nuptials of Pirithous with Hippodamia, the daughter of Adrastus, king of Argos. The Centaurs also attended the festivity, and quarreled with the Lapithæ, which resulted in blows and slaughter. Many of the Centaurs were slain, and they were at last obliged to retire.

LA'RES. Gods of inferior power at Rome, who presided over houses and families. They were divided into two classes.

LATI'NUS. A son of Faunus and the nymph Marica, king of the Aborigines in Italy, who from him were called Latini.

LATI'UM. A district in Italy inhabited by the Latini. It contained Rome and was the heart of the Roman dominion.

LATO'NA. A daughter of Cœus, the Titan, and Phœbe. She was admired for her beauty by Jupiter. Juno made Latona the object of her vengeance, and sent the serpent Python to persecute her.

LEAN'DER. A youth of Abydos. He was passionately in love with Hero, a young girl of Sestos. He was in the habit of swimming across the Hellespont to visit her, in doing which, on a tempestuous night, he was drowned. Byron performed the same feat in 1810, an exploit which he has celebrated in verse in his occasional pieces. He expresses surprise that, as the truth of Leander's story had been questioned, no one had hitherto tested its practicability.

LE'DA. A daughter of King Thestius and Eurythemis, who married Tyndarus, king of Sparta. She is famous for her intrigue with Jupiter (Zeus), who came to her in the form of a swan. She brought forth two eggs, from one of which sprung Pollux and Helena, and from the other Castor and Clytemnestra. She is said to have received the name of Nemesis after death.

LEM'NOS. One of the largest islands in the Ægaean sea. It was sacred to Vulcan (Hephaestus), who is said to have fallen there when Jupiter hurled him from Olympus.

LEM'URES. The manes of the dead. The ancients supposed that after death the departed souls wandered over the world and disturbed the peace of its inhabitants.

LEON'IDAS. A celebrated king of Sparta who went to oppose Xerxes, king of Persia, who had invaded Greece with a vast army. A battle was fought at Thermopylæ, the entire army of Leonidas consisting of 300 men who refused to abandon him. For a time this small army resisted the vast legions of Xerxes, till at length a traitor conducted a detachment of Persians by a secret path to the rear of Leonidas, when his soldiers were cut to pieces, one only of the 300 escaping.

LEP'IDUS, M. ÆMIL'IUS. A celebrated Roman, one of the triumvirs with Augustus and Antony. He was of an illustrious family, and, like many of his contemporaries, remarkable for ambition. He was unable to maintain his position as triumvir, and, resigning power, he sank into obscurity. Died B. C. 13.

LES'BOS. The largest and most important of the islands in the Ægaean Sea.

LE'THE. One of the rivers of hell, whose waters were imbibed by the souls of the dead which had been for a certain period confined in Tartarus. Those who drank of this river forgot whatever they had previously known. In this sense the word is constantly used by the poets. Thus Shakspeare (Henry IV) says:—

"May this be washed in Lethe and forgotten."

LE'TO, called Latona by the Romans, was the wife of Jupiter (Zeus) and the mother of Apollo and Diana (Artemis).

LEUCIP'PUS. A celebrated philosopher of Abdera, about 428 years before Christ. He was a disciple of Zeno. His life was written by Diogenes. There were several others of the same name.

LEUCOTH'EA. The name of Ino after she was transformed into a sea-nymph.

LEUC'TRA. A village in Bœotia, famous for the victory which Epaminondas, the Theban general, obtained over the superior force of Cleombrotus, king of Sparta, B. C. 371.

LEVA'NA. The deity who presided over new-born infants.

LIB'ISSA. Queen of fays and fairies.

LIBITI'NA. The chief of the funeral deities.

LICIN'IUS, C. A tribune of the people celebrated for his intrigues and ability. He was a plebeian, and was the first of that class that was raised to the office of master of the horse to the dictator. There were a number of other Romans of the same name.

LI'LITH. A Jewish myth who is a great enemy to new-born children. She was said to have been Adam's first wife, but, refusing to submit to him, was turned from Paradise and made a spectre.

LI'NA. The goddess of the art of weaving.

LIN'DOR. A lover in the shape of a shepherd, like Corydon; a love-sick swain.

LIV'IUS, TI'TUS. A native of Padua, a celebrated historian. He passed the chief part of his time at Naples and Rome, but more particularly at the court at Augustus, who liberally patronized him. The name of Livy is rendered immortal by his history of the Roman empire. The merit of this history is admitted by all, and the high rank which Livy holds among historians is undisputed. He died A.D. 17. Of his immortal history in 142 books, only 35 are extant. He was the greatest of the Roman historians.

LIV'IUS ANDRONI'CUS was a dramatic poet who flourished at Rome about 240 years before the Christian era; the first Latin author of any note; sometimes called the father of Latin literature.

LO'FEN. The Scandinavian god who guards friendship.

LOF'UA. The Scandinavian goddess who reconciles lovers.

LOKE. The Scandinavian Satan, the god of strife, the spirit of evil.

LONGI'NUS, DIONYS'IUS CAS'SIUS. A celebrated Greek philosopher of Athens. He was preceptor of the Greek language, and afterwards minister to Zenobia, the famous queen of Palmyra. He was killed B. C. 273.

LO'TIS. Daughter of Neptune, who fled from Priapus, and only escaped from him by being transformed into a lotus-plant.

LUCA'NUS, M. ANNÆ'US. A native of Corduba in Spain. At an early age he went to Rome, where his rising talents recommended him to the emperor Nero. He unwisely entered into a poetical contest with Nero, in which he obtained an easy victory, which greatly offended the emperor. After this Lucan was exposed to much annoyance from Nero, and was induced to join in a conspiracy against him, on which he was condemned to death, the mode of which he had the liberty of choosing. He decided to have his veins opened in a warm bath, and died quoting some lines from his "Pharsalia." Of all his works none but the "Pharsalia" remains. He is commonly called Lucan.

LUCIA'NUS. A celebrated writer of Samosata. His works are numerous, consisting chiefly of dialogues written with much force. He died A. D. 180, being, as some say, torn in pieces by dogs for his impiety. He is always called Lucian.

LU'CIFER. The name of the planet Venus, or morning star. It is called Lucifer when appearing in the morning before the sun, but when it appears after its setting it is called Hesperus.

LUCIL'IUS, C. A Roman knight, who is regarded as the first satirical writer among the Romans. Of thirty satires which he wrote only a few verses remain. He died at Naples, B. C. 103.

LUCIL'IUS LUCI'NUS. A famous Roman who fled with Brutus from the battle of Phillippi. He was taken prisioner, but the conquerors spared his life.

LUCI'NA. Daughter of Jupiter (Zeus) and Juno (Hera). She was the goddess who presided over the birth of children.

LUCRE'TIA. A celebrated Roman lady, daughter of Lucretius and wife of Tarquinius Collatinus. A number of young noble Romans at Ardea, among whom were Collatinus and the sons of Tarquin the Proud, were discussing the virtues of their wives at home, and it was agreed to go to Rome to ascertain how their wives employed themselves in their husbands' absence in the camp. While the wives of the others were indulging in feasting and dissipation, Lucretia was found in her house employing herself with her servants in domestic duties. She was brutally treated by Sextus Tarquin, a relative of Collatinus, and stabbed herself. This was the signal for a rebellion, the result being the expulsion of the Tarquins rrom Rome. See Shakspeare's "Lucrece."

LUCRE'TIUS, CA'RUS T. A celebrated Roman poet and philosopher. The tenets of Epicurus were embraced by him, and were explained and elucidated in a poem which he wrote, *De rerum natura*. This poem is distinguished by genius and elegance, but the doctrines it inculcates have an atheistical tendency. Lucretius is said to have destroyed himself B. C. 54.

LUCUS'TA. A woman celebrated for her skill in concocting poisons. She was employed by Agrippina in poisoning the Roman Emperor Claudius, and by Nero for getting rid of Brittanicus.

LUCUL'LUS, LU'CIUS LICIN'IUS. A Roman noted for his fondness of luxury and for his military abilities. He was born about 115 years before the Christian era, and distinguished himself by his proficiency in eloquence and philosophy. He was soon advanced to the consulship, and entrusted with the management of the Mithridatic war, in which he displayed his military talents.

LUD. In ancient British mythology the king of the Britons.

LU'NA. The name of Diana as a celestial divinity. See Diana and Hecate.

LU'PERCUS, or PAN. The Roman god of fertility; his festival day was 15th February, and the festivals were called Lupercalia.

LYCAON'IAN FOOD. Execrable viands, such as were supplied to Jupiter by Lycaon. To test the divine knowledge of the god he served up human flesh, which Jove discovered, and punished Lycaon by turning him into a wolf.

LUS'CIUS, L. A Latin comic poet, a contemporary and rival of Terence.

LYCUR'GUS. A celebrated lawgiver of Sparta, son of King Eunomus and brother to Polydectes. He succeeded his brother on the Spartan throne. In the laws which he enacted he maintained a just equilibrium between the throne and the people; he banished luxury and encouraged the useful arts, and adopted a number of measures having for their object the well-being of the people.

LYD'IA. A district of Asia Minor; it bordered on the Ægaean Sea.

LYN'CEUS, son of Aphareus, was one of the hunters of the Calydonian boar, and one of the Argonauts. He was so sharp-sighted that he could see through the earth and distinguish objects at a great distance from him. There was another person of the same name who married Hypermnestra, daughter of Danaus.

LYSAN'DER. A celebrated general of Sparta in the last years of the Peloponnesian war. He drew Ephesus from the interest of Athens, and gained the friendship of Cyrus the Younger. He gave battle to the Athenian fleet, and destroyed it all except three ships. In this battle, which was fought 405 years before the Christian era, the Athenians lost a great number of men, and in consequence of it forfeited their influence over neighboring states. Lysander was killed in battle 394 years B. C.

LYSIM'ACHUS. A son of Agathocles, who was one of the generals of Alexander. After the death of that monarch Lysimachus made himself master of Thrace, where he built a town which he called Lysimachia.

LYSIP'PUS. A famous sculptor of Sicyon. He applied himself to painting, but he was born to excel in sculpture. He lived about 325 years before the Christian era, in the age of Alexander the Great.

M

MACRO'BIUS. A Latin writer who died A. D. 415. He has rendered himself famous for a composition called *Saturnalia*, a miscellaneous collection of antiquarian and critical literature.

MÆAN'DER. A celebrated river of Asia Minor flowing into the Ægaean Sea. It is famous among the poets for its windings, and from it the application of the word "meandering" to a winding stream has become proverbial.

MA'ECENAS, or MECA'ENAS, C. CILNIUS, a celebrated Roman knight, has rendered himself immortal by his liberal patronage of learned men. He was a great friend of the Emperor Augustus and took part in affairs of state. To the interference of Maecenas Virgil was indebted for the restitution of his lands. Maecenas, according to the received opinion, wrote a history of animals and a journal of the life of Augustus. Virgil dedicated his Georgics to him, as did Horace his Odes. He died B. C. 8.

MAG'I. An order of priests among the Medes and Persians. They also discharged judicial functions.

MAGNE'SIA. A city in Lydia in Asia Minor famous as the scene of the defeat of Antiochus the Great, by the two Scipios B. C. 190.

MA'NES. A name applied by the ancients to the soul when departed from the body.

MAN'LIUS, MAR'CUS. A celebrated Roman who, at an early age, distinguished himself for valor. When Rome was taken by the Gauls, he, with a body of his countrymen, fled to the capitol, which he defended when it was surprised in the night by the enemy. This gained him the surname of *Capitolinus*, and the geese which had awakened him to action by their clamor were afterwards held sacred among the Romans.

MAR'ATHON. A village of Attica, celebrated for the victory which the Athenians and Platæans, under the command of Miltiades, gained over the Persian army, 490 B. C.

MARCEL'LUS, MAR'CUS CLAU'DIUS. 1 A famous Roman general. He was the first Roman who obtained any advantage over Hannibal. He conquered Syracuse, with the spoils from which he adorned Rome. He was killed in battle in his fifth consulship B. C. 208. 2 A Roman who distinguished himself in the civil wars of Cæsar and Pompey by his firm attachment to the latter. He was banished by Cæsar, but was afterwards recalled at the request of the senate. Pope ("Essay on Man,") has a couplet referring to him:—

"And more true joy Marcellus exil'd feels,
Than Cæsar with a senate at his heels."

There were some other Romans of the name, of minor repute.

MARDO'NIUS. A general in the army of Xerxes who was defeated in the battle of Platæa, where he was slain B. C. 479.

MARI'NA. A name of Venus, meaning sea-foam, from her having been formed from the froth of the sea.

MA'RIUS, C. A celebrated Roman who signalized himself under Scipio at the siege of Numantia. He was appointed to finish the war against Jugurtha, who was defeated and betrayed into the hands of the Romans. After this new honors awaited Marius. He was elected consul, and was sent against the Teutones. The war was prolonged, and Marius was a third and fourth time invested with the consulship. At length two engagements were fought, and the Teutones were defeated, a vast number of them being left dead on the battle-fields. The contest for supremacy between himself and Sulba was the cause of the great civil war. After many vicissitudes Marius died, B. C. 86, directly after he had been honored with the consulship for the seventh time. There were a number of others of the same name, but of minor note.

MARS (Ares), the god of war, was the son of Jupiter and Juno, or of Juno alone, according to Ovid. The loves of Mars and Venus are greatly celebrated. On one occasion while in each other's company, Vulcan spread a net round them, from which they could not escape without assistance. They were thus exposed to the ridicule of the gods till Neptune induced Vulcan to set them at liberty. During the Trojan war Mars interested himself on the side of the Trojans, and

Mars.

defended the favorites of Venus with great determination. He was principally worshipped as the god of war, and as such bore the epithet Gradivus; but he was also regarded as the patron of agriculture, which procured him the title of Silvanus; and as the patron of the state, in virtue of which he was called Quirinus. In works of art Mars is generally represented as of a youthful but powerful figure, armed with the helmet, shield and spear. At other times he is bearded and heavily armed.

MAR'SYAS. A celebrated piper of Celæne in Phrygia. He challenged Apollo to a trial of skill in music, which challenge was accepted, the Muses being appointed umpires. The palm of victory was awarded to Apollo, who tied his antagonist to a tree and flayed him. His blood was the source of the river Marlzas.

Martia'lis, Mar'cus Vale'rius. A native of Spain who came to Rome when he was about twenty years old, where he became noticeable by his poetical genius. Martial wrote fourteen books of epigrams, and died in the seventy-fifth year of his age, 104 A. D.

Masinis'sa. A king of Numidia, a small part of Africa, who at first assisted the Carthaginians in their wars against Rome, but who suddenly became an ally to the Romans. After his defeat of Syphax he married Sophonisba, the wife of Syphax, which gave offence to the Roman general Scipio, on which Masinissa induced Sophonisba to end her life by poison. In the battle of Zama, Masinissa greatly contributed to the defeat of Hannibal. He died in his ninety-seventh year, 149 B. C.

Mauretan'ia, the westernmost of the divisions of Northern Africa. It became a Roman province A. D. 40. Its ancient inhabitants still exist in powerful tribes in Morocco and Algiers.

Mauso'lus. A king of Caria. His wife Artemisia was very disconsolate at his death, and erected one of the grandest monuments of antiquity to perpetuate his memory. This famous building, which was deemed to be one of the seven wonders of the world, was called "Mausoleum," which name has been since applied to other grand sepulchral monuments.

Maximi'nus, Ca'ius Ju'lius Ve'rus, was the son of a peasant of Thrace. He entered the Roman armies, where he gradually rose till he was proclaimed emperor A. D. 235. He ruled with great cruelty, and was eventually killed by his own soldiers. He was of immense size and strength, and was able to break the hardest stones between his fingers.

Mede'a. A celebrated magician, daughter of Ætes, king of Colchis, and niece of Circe. When Jason came to Colchis in quest of the Golden Fleece, Medea fell in love with him, and they exchanged oaths of fidelity, and when he had overcome the difficulties which he had to encounter, Medea embarked with him for Greece. She lived in Corinth with her husband Jason for ten years, with much conjugal happiness, when he became enamored with

Glauce, daughter of Creon, king of Corinth. To avenge herself on Jason she caused the destruction of Glauce, and killed her two children in his presence.

MEDU'SA. One of the three Gorgons, daughter of Phorcys and Ceto. She was the only one of the Gorgons subject to mortality. She was celebrated for her personal charms and the beauty of her hair, which Minerva changed into serpents. According to Apollodorus and others, the Gorgons were born with snakes on their heads instead of hair, and with yellow wings, and brazen hands. Perseus rendered himself famous by his conquest of Medusa. He cut off her head and placed it on the ægis of Minerva. The head had the power of changing those who looked at it into stone. Medusa, as we are informed by Lord Lytton, was an expression applied to Mary Queen of Scots in her own day, and in his brilliant poem, "The Last Days of Queen Elizabeth," he speaks of the unfortunate queen as:—

"Thou soft Medusa of the fated line.

MELEA'GER. A celebrated hero of antiquity who signalized himself in the Argonautic expedition, and especially by killing the Calydonian boar, a famous event in mythological history.

ME'LOS. An island in the Ægaean Sea.

MELPOM'ENE. One of the Muses, daughter of Jupiter and Mnemosyne. She presided over tragedy. She is generally represented as a young woman wearing a buskin, with vine leaves surrounding her head, and holding in her hand a tragic mask.

MELLO'NA. One of the rural divinities, the goddess of bees.

MEM'NON. A king of Ethiopia, son of Tithonus and Aurora. He came with ten thousand men to assist Priam in the Trojan war, where he behaved with great courage, and killed Antilochus, Nestor's son, on which Nestor challenged Memnon to fight, but he refused on account of the great age of the challenger; but he fought Achilles, who killed him. A

Melpomene — Antique in the Vatican.

statue was erected in his honor which had the property of uttering a melodious sound every day at sunrise. Tennyson, in his " Palace of Art," alludes to this statue thus:

> "As morn from Memnon drew
> Rivers of melodies."

MENAN'DER. A celebrated comic poet of Athens, educated under Theophrastus. He was universally esteemed by the Greeks. He wrote 108 comedies, but of which only a few fragments remain. He died B. C. 291.

MEN'DES. An Egyptian god like Pan. He was worshipped in the form of a goat.

MENELA'US. A king of Sparta, brother of Agamemnon. He married Helen, the most beautiful woman of her time. Paris, having arrived in Sparta in the absence of Menelaus, persuaded her to elope with him, which was the cause of the Trojan war. In the tenth year of the war Helen, it is said, obtained the forgiveness of Menelaus, with whom she returned to Sparta, where, shortly after his return, he died.

MENE'NIUS AGRIP'PA. A celebrated Roman who appeased the Roman populace in the infancy of the consular government by repeating to them the well-known fable of the belly and limbs. He lived B. C. 495.

MENIP'PUS. A Cynic philosopher of Phœnicia. He was originally a slave, and, obtaining his liberty, became notoricus as a usurer. He wrote thirteen books of satires. He flourished about B. C. 60.

MEN'TOR. A faithful friend of Ulysses, and guide and instructor of his son Telemachus. The term Mentor has become proverbial as applied to any one who is an educator of youth.

MER'OPE. One of the Atlantides. She married Sisyphus, son of Æolus, and was changed into a constellation.

ME'ROPS. A king of the island of Cos, who married Clymene, one of the Oceanides. He was changed into an eagle, and placed among the constellations.

ME'RU. The abode of the Hindoo god Vishnu. It is at the top of a mountain 80,000 leagues high. The Olympus of the Indians.

MERCU'RY. A celebrated god of antiquity, called Hermes by the Greeks. He was the messenger of the gods, and conducted the souls of the dead into the infernal regions. He presided over orators, merchants, and was also the god of thieves. The invention of the lyre is ascribed to him. This he gave to Apollo, and received in exchange the Caduceus, which the god of poetry used to drive the flocks of King Admetus. He was also the messenger, herald, and ambassador of Jupiter. As a Roman divinity he was merely the patron of commerce and gain. Mercury was accounted a most cunning thief, for he stole the bow and quiver of Apollo, the girdle of Venus, the trident of Neptune, the tools of Vulcan, and the sword of Mars, and he was therefore called the god of thieves. There was also an Egyptian Mercury, under the name of Thot, who is credited with having taught the Egyptians geometry and hieroglyphics.

Mercury.

MESSALI'NA VALE'RIA, was notorious for her vices. She married the Emperor Claudius, who, wearied with her misconduct, cited her to appear before him and reply to the accusations which were brought against her, on which she attempted to destroy herself, but failing to do so, was slain by one of the tribunes who had been sent to summon her

METEL'LI. The surname of a family of the Cæcilii at Rome, the most noted of whom are—a general who defeated the Achæans, took Thebes, and invaded Macedonia; Quintus Cæcilius, rendered famous by his successes against Jugurtha, the king of Numidia; Q. Cæcilius Celer, who distinguished himself against Catiline. He died fifty-seven years before Christ, greatly lamented by Cicero, who was one of his warmest friends; L. Cæcilius, a tribune in the civil wars of Cæsar and Pompey who favored the cause of Pompey; Q. Cæcilius, a warlike general who conquered Crete and Macedonia; Metellus Cimber, one of the conspirators against Cæsar. He gave the signal to attack and murder the dictator.

ME'TIS. The personification of prudence, daughter of Oceanus and Tethys, and first wife of Jupiter (Zeus). Was destroyed by him.

MICIP'SA. A king of Numidia, son of Masinissa, who at his death, B. C. 119, left his kingdom between his sons, Adherbal and Hiempsal, and his nephew Jugurtha.

MI'DAS. A king of Phrygia, son of Gordius or Gorgias. According to some traditions, in the early part of his life he found a treasure, to which he owed his greatness and opulence. He showed hospitality to Silenus, in return for which Bacchus permitted him to choose whatever recompense he pleased. He demanded of the god that whatever he touched might be turned into gold. His wish was granted, but when the very food which he attempted to eat became gold in his mouth, he prayed Bacchus to revoke the favor, and he was ordered to wash himself in the river Pactolus, the sands of which were turned into gold by the touch of Midas. Afterwards, in consequence of maintaining that Pan was superior to Apollo in singing and playing the flute, he had his ears changed into those of an ass by the god.

MI'LO. 1. A celebrated athlete of Crotona in Italy. He is said to have carried on his shoulders a bullock for a considerable distance, and to have killed it with a blow from his fist, and eaten it in one day. In his old age he attempted to pull up a tree by the roots, which, when half cleft, reunited, and his hands remaining imprisoned in the tree, he was eaten by wild beasts about 500 years before the Christian era.

MILO. 2. T. Armius Milo Pepricanus, a Roman of unscrupulous character. He had a prolonged contest with P. Clodius for the consulship of Rome in 53 B. C. In an affray he killed Clodius, was accused of the crime, and defended by Cicero in one of his most famous orations. He was exiled.

MILTI'ADES, son of Simon, was sent by the Athenians to take possession of the Chersonesus. On his arrival he seized some of the principal inhabitants of the country, made himself absolute in Chersonese, and married the daughter of Olorus, king of the Thracians. He was present at the celebrated battle of Marathon, where the command was ceded to him, owing to his superior abilities. He obtained the victory, but an olive crown, which he demanded from his fellow citizens as a reward for his valor, was refused. Afterwards he was entrusted with a fleet of seventy ships, with which to punish some islands which had revolted to the Persians. At first he was successful, but afterwards fortune frowned on him. He was accused of treason and condemned to death, but his sentence was, owing to his great services, commuted. He died in prison of some wounds he had received which became incurable.

MINER'VA (Athena), the goddess of wisdom, war, and all the liberal arts, sprang, full-grown and armed, from the head of Jupiter, and was immediately admitted to the assembly of the gods, and became one of the most faithful counsellors of her father. Her power in heaven was great; she could hurl the thunders of Jupiter, prolong the life of men, and bestow the gift of prophecy. She was known among the ancients by many names. She was called Athena, Pallas, Parthenos, Tritonia (because she was worshipped near the lake Tritonis), and Hippia (because she first taught mankind how to manage the horse), Sais (because she was worshipped at Sais), and some other names. She was the patroness of all the arts and trades. She is said to have invented numbers. The number five is sacred to Minerva. She is usually represented with a helmet on her head with a large plume on it, in one hand holding a spear, and in the other a shield with the head of Medusa on it. Temples were erected for her worship in different places, one of the most renowned of which was the Parthenon at Athens. From this building a large collection of ancient sculpture was brought to the British Museum by Lord Elgin more than sixty years ago, which is known as the "Elgin Marbles."

MI'NOS. A king of Crete, son of Jupiter and Europa, who gave laws to his subjects B. C. 1406, which remained in full force in the age of Plato. After death became a judge of the Shades in Hades. His grandson of the same name, was the husband of Pasiphæ.

MINOTAU'RUS. A celebrated monster, half a man and half a bull, for which a number of young Athenian men and maidens were yearly exacted to be devoured. The Minotaur was confined in a famous labyrinth, where at length it was slain by Theseus, who was guided out of the labyrinth by a clue of thread given to him by Ariadne, daughter of King Minos.

MITH'RA. A Persian divinity, that ruled the universe, corresponding with the Roman Sol.

MITHRIDA'TES FIRST, king of Pontus. He was tributary to the crown of Persia; his attempts to make himself independent of that fealty proved fruitless, being defeated in battle which he had provoked, and having to sue for peace.

MITHRIDA'TES, surnamed "Eupator" and "The Great," succeeded to the throne of Pontus when eleven years of age. The beginning of his reign was marked by ambition and cruelty. At an early age he inured himself to hardships by devoting himself to manly exercises, and sleeping in the open air on the bare earth. He was constantly engaged in warfare against the Romans, and his contests with them are known as the Mithridatic wars. His hatred of the Romans was so great that, to destroy their power, he ordered all of them that were in his dominions to be massacred; and in one night 150,000, according to Plutarch, or 80,000 according to another authority, were slaughtered. This cruel act called for revenge, and great armies were sent against him. After varied fortunes Mithridates had to succumb to Pompey, and, worn out with misfortune, attempted to poison himself, but unsuccessfully, and the numerous antidotes to poison which in early life he had taken, strengthened his constitution to resist the effect. He then ordered one of his soldiers to give him the fatal blow with a sword, which was done. He died about sixty-three years before the Christian era, in his seventy-second year. He is said to have been the most formidable opponent the Romans ever had, and Cicero estimates him as the greatest monarch that ever sat upon a throne. It is recorded of him that he conquered twenty-four nations, whose different languages he knew and spoke fluently. There were a number of persons of the same name, but of inferior note.

MNEMOS'YNE (Memory). A daughter of Cœlus and Terra, mother of the nine Muses. Jupiter assumed the form of a shepherd in order to enjoy her company.

MOAK'IBAT. The recording angel of the Mohammedans.

MOER'Æ, called Parcae by Romans. They were the Fates, three in number. Clotho, or the spinning fate Lachesis, or the one who assigns to man his fate, and Atropos, or, the fate that cannot be avoided.

MO'LOCH. A god of the Phœnicians to whom human victims, principally children, were sacrificed. Moloch is figurative of the influence which impels us to sacrifice that which we ought to cherish most dearly.

"First Moloch, horrid king, besmeared with blood
Of human sacrifice, and parents' tears,
Though for the noise of drums and timbrels loud,
Their children's cries unheard, that poured through fire
To this grim idol."   MILTON.

MO'MUS, the god of mirth among the ancients, according to Hesiod, was the son of Nox. He amused himself by satirizing the gods by turning into ridicule whatever they did.

MONE'TA. A name given to Juno by those writers who considered her the goddess of money.

MOON. The moon was, by the ancients, called *Hecate* before and after setting, *Astarte* when in crescent form, *Diana* when in full.

MOR'PHEUS. A minister of the god Somnus, who imitated very naturally the gestures, words and manners of mankind. He is the son of the god of sleep. He is generally represented as a sleeping child, of great corpulence, with wings. He is said to shape our dreams.

MOS'CHUS. A Greek Bucolic poet in the age of Ptolemy Philadelphus. His eclogues are characterized by sweetness and elegance; B. C. 250.

MUN'IN. The Scandinavian god of memory, represented by the raven that was perched on Odin's shoulder.

MURE'NA, L. A celebrated Roman, who invaded the dominions of Mithridates, at first with success, but afterwards he met with defeat. He was honored with a triumph on his return to Rome; B. C. 81.

MU'SÆ. The Muses, certain goddesses who presided over poetry, music, dancing, and all the liberal arts. They were daughters of Jupiter and Mnemosyne, born at Piesia, and were nine in number, Clio, Euterpe, Thalia, Melpomene, Terpsichore, Erato, Polyhymnia, Calliope, and Urania.

MUSCA'RIUS. A name given to Jupiter because he kept off the flies from the sacrifices.

MYCE'NÆ. A town of Argolis said to have been built by Perseus. It received its name from Mycene, a nymph of Laconia. It was taken and destroyed by the Argives.

N

NAI'ADES. Nymphs or inferior deities who presided over rivers, springs, wells and fountains. The Naiads generally inhabited the country, and resorted to the woods and meadows near the stream over which they presided. They are represented as young and beautiful girls leaning on an urn, from which flows a stream of water. Ægle was the fairest of them, according to Virgil. The word Naiad has become Anglicised, and is in frequent use, especially by the poets. Thus Scott says, in his "Lady of the Lake":—

> "In listening mood she seem'd to stand
> The guardian Naiad of the strand."

NAN'DI. The Hindoo goddess of joy.

NAR'DE. The name of the infernal regions among the Hindoos.

NA'RA'YAN. The mover of the waters. The Hindoo god of tides.

NARCIS'SUS. A beautiful youth, son of Cephisus and the nymph Liriope, was born at Thespis in Bœotia. He saw his image reflected in a fountain and became in love with it, thinking it to be the nymph of the place. His fruitless attempts to reach this beautiful object so provoked him, that he killed himself. His blood was changed into a flower which still bears his name.

NASTR'OND. The Scandinavian place of eternal punishment, corresponding with Hades.

NAUSI'CÆ. Daughter of Alcinous, king of Phæacians, who conducted Ulysses to the Court of her father when he was shipwrecked on the coast. (Odyssey.)

NEMÆ'A. A town of Argolis, with a wood where Hercules in the sixteenth year of his age killed the celebrated Nemæan lion. It was the first of the labors of Hercules to destroy the monster, and when he found that his arrows and clubs were useless against an animal whose skin was impenetrable, he seized it in his arms and strangled it.

NEM'ESIS. One of the infernal deities, daughter of Nox. She was the goddess of vengeance. She is made one of the Parcæ by some mythologists, and is represented with a helm and a wheel. The term is sometimes used to signify vengeance itself.

NEOPTOL'EMUS. A king of Epirus, son of Achilles and Deidamia, called also Pyrrhus. He greatly signalized himself during the siege of Troy, and he was the first who entered the wooden horse. He was inferior to none of the Grecian warriors in valor. Ulysses and Nestor alone were his superiors in eloquence and wisdom.

NEP'TUNE (Poseidon). One of the gods, son of Saturn and Ops, and brother to Jupiter and Pluto. He was devoured by his father as soon as he was born, and restored to life again by a potion given to Saturn, by Metis, the first wife of Jupiter. Neptune shared with his brothers the empire of Saturn, and received as his portion the kingdom of the sea. He did not think this equivalent to the empire of heaven and earth, which Jupiter had claimed, therefore he conspired to dethrone him. The conspiracy was discovered, and Jupiter condemned Neptune to build the walls of Troy. He married Amphitrite, who thus broke a vow she had made of perpetual celibacy.

Neptune.

The chief marine divinity of the Romans, hence identified by the Romans themselves with the Greek Poseidon, whose attributes they transferred to their own god. In works of art he is usually represented as armed with a trident, and the horse and the dolphin are his symbols. Though a marine deity, he was reputed to have presided over horse training and horse races; but he is principally known as the god of the ocean; and the two functions of the god are portrayed in the sea-horses with which his chariot is drawn, the fore half of the animal being a horse, and the hind half a dolphin. Ships were also under his protection, and whenever he appeared on the ocean there was a dead calm.

NE'POS, CORNE'LIUS. A celebrated historian in the reign of Augustus, and, like the rest of his literary contemporaries, he enjoyed the patronage and obtained the favor of the emperor. He was the intimate friend of Cicero and Atticus, and recommended himself to notice by delicacy of sentiment and a lively disposition. Of all his valuable works the only one extant is his Lives of illustrious Greek and Roman generals.

NERE'IDES. Nymphs of the sea, daughters of Nereus and Doris. According to most of the mythologists, they were fifty in number. They are represented as young and handsome girls, sitting on dolphins and armed with tridents. In ancient monuments the Nereids are represented as riding on sea-horses, sometimes with the human form entire, and sometimes with the tail of a fish. They constantly attended Neptune.

NERE'US. A sea deity, god of the Mediterranean, husband of Doris. He had the gift of prophecy, and foretold fates: but he had also the power of assuming various shapes, which enabled him to escape from the importunities of those who were anxious to consult him.

NE'RO, CLAU'DIUS, DOMIT'IUS CÆ'SAR. A celebrated Roman emperor, son of Caius Domitius Ahenobarbus and Agrippina, the daughter of Germanicus. His name is the synonym for cruelty and vice. In the night it was his wont to sally out from his palace to visit the meanest taverns and the different scenes of depravity that were to be found.

He appeared on the stage, sometimes representing the meanest characters. He resolved to imitate the burning of Troy, and caused Rome to be set on fire in different places, the flames being unextinguished for nine days, and he enjoyed the terrible scene. During the conflagration he placed himself on the top of a tower and sang, accompanying himself on a lyre, of the destruction of Troy. Many conspiracies were formed against him, the most dangerous of which he was saved from by the confession of a slave. He killed himself A. D. 68, in the thirty-second year of his age, after a reign of thirteen years and eight months. Wretch that he was, it is said that he had some few to mourn for him, and Suetonius records that some unseen hand had placed flowers on his tomb.

NER'VA, M. COCCE'IUS. A Roman emperor after the death of Domitian, A. D. 96. He rendered himself popular by his mildness and generosity. In his civil character he set an example of good manners and sobriety. He made an oath that no senator should suffer death during his reign, which he carried out by pardoning two members of the senate who had conspired against his life. He died in his sixty-fifth year, A. D. 98, and was succeeded by his son Trajan.

NES'SUS. A celebrated Centaur killed by Hercules for insulting Dejanira.

NES'TOR. A son of Neleus and Chloris, nephew to Pellas, and grandson to Neptune, husband of Eurydice. He was present at the bloody battle between the Lapithæ and the Centaurs, which took place at the nuptials of Pirithous. As king of Pylos he led his soldiers to the Trojan war, where he distinguished himself among the Grecian chieftains by eloquence, wisdom, and prudence. Homer makes his character as the most perfect of all the heroes. After the Trojan war Nestor retired to Greece, where he lived during his declining years in peace and tranquility. The manner and time of his death are unknown.

NID'HOGG. In Scandinavian mythology the dragon who dwells in Nastrond.

NIF'LHEIM. The Scandinavian hell. It was supposed to

consist of nine vast regions of ice beneath the North Pole, where darkness reigns eternally.

NI'KE. Called Victoria by the Romans, the goddess of victory. Daughter of Pallas and Styx, sister of Zeleus (zeal), Cretor (strength), and Bia (force). When Jupiter (Zeus) commenced fighting against the Titans, she and her sisters were the first of the gods to come to his aid. She had a celebrated temple on the Acropolis of Athens, the ruins of which are extant. In art her appearance resembles that of Minerva, but has wings and carries a palm or wreath, and a shield.

NI'LUS. The god of the River Nile, son of Oceanus and Tethys. Pindar calls him the son of Saturn (Chronos).

NI'NUS. A son of Belus. He built Nineveh and founded the Assyrian monarchy, of which he was the first sovereign, B. C. 2059. He married Semiramis, whose husband had destroyed himself through fear of Ninus. He reigned fifty-two years.

NI'OBE. A daughter of Tantalus, king of Lydia, and Euryanassa, or Dione. She married Amphion, and, according to Hesiod, they had ten sons and ten daughters. All the sons of Niobe expired by the darts of Apollo, and all the daughters, except Chloris, were destroyed by Diana (Artemis), for her presumption in thinking herself superior to Latona, who had only two children. She herself was metamorphosed by Zeus (Jupiter) into a stone which shed tears during the summer. This fable has afforded a subject for art, and has given rise to the beautiful group in the tribune at Florence, known by the name of Niobe and her Children.

Niobe—Antique, Florence.

NITO'CRIS. A celebrated queen of Babylon, who built a bridge across the Euphrates in the middle of that city, and dug a number of reservoirs for the superfluous water of the river. She was the wife of Nebuchadnezzar, mother of Belshazzar.

NOM'ADES. A name given to people who had no fixed habitation, and who continually changed their place of residence in quest of fresh pastures for the cattle they tended. There were Nomades in Scythia, India, Arabia, etc. The word is in constant use as Anglicised—Nomad—meaning any one who leads a wandering and unsettled life.

No'MIUS. A lawgiver; one of the names of Apollo. This title was also given to Mercury for the part he took in inventing beneficient laws. It is a surname given to divinities protecting pastures and shepherds.

NORNS. Three Scandinavian goddesses, who wove the woof of human destiny.

No'TUS. Another name for Auster, the south wind.

NOX or NYX. One of the most ancient deities among the heathens, daughter of Chaos. She gave birth to the Day and the Light, and was mother of the Parcæ, Hesperides, Dreams, Death, etc.

NU'MA POMPIL'IUS. A celebrated philosopher of Cures. He married Tatia, daughter of Tatius, king of the Sabines, and at her death he retired into the country to devote himself to literary pursuits. At the death of Romulus the Romans fixed on him to be their new king. Numa at first refused the offer of the crown, but at length was prevailed on to accept it. He endeavored to inculcate into the minds of his subjects a reverence for the deity, and he did all he could to heal their dissensions. He encouraged the report of his visits to the nymph Egeria, and made use of her name to give sanction to the laws which he had made. He dedicated a temple to Janus, which, during his whole reign, remained closed as a mark of peace and tranquility at Rome. Numa died after a reign of forty-three years (B. C. 672), during which he had given encouragement to the useful arts, and had cultivated peace.

NUMID'IA. A country of Northern Africa, the country of Masinissa and Jugurtha.

NYCTE'LIUS. A name given to Bacchus, because his festivals were celebrated by torchlight.

NYM'PHÆ. Certain female deities of low rank, the daughter of Jupiter (Zeus). They were generally divided into two classes—nymphs of the land and nymphs of the sea. Of the former some presided over woods, and were called Dryades and Hamadryades. Of the sea nymphs some were called Oceanides, Nereides, Naiades, etc. They were thought to be endowed with prophetic power, and to inspire men with the same, and to confer upon them the gift of poetry.

NY'SÆUS. A name of Bacchus, because he was worshipped at Nysa.

NY'SUS. A king of Megara who was invisible by virtue of a particular lock of hair.

O

OAN'NES. An Eastern god, represented as a monster, half man, half fish. He was said to have taught men the use of letters in the day-time, and at night to have retired to the depth of the sea.

OCEAN'IDES. Sea nymphs, daughters of Oceanus, from whom they received their name. According to Apollodorus they were 3,000 in number, while Hesiod speaks of them as consisting of forty-one. See Nymphæ.

OCE'ANUS. A powerful deity of the sea, son of Cœlus and Terra. He married Tethys, the Oceanides being their children. Father of all the river gods.

OCTA'VIA. A Roman lady, sister to the Emperor Augustus, celebrated for her beauty and virtues. She married Claudius Marcellus, and, after his death, Antony, who for some time was attentive to her, but eventually deserted her for Cleopatra. Died B. C. 11.

OCTAVIA'NUS, or OCTA'VIUS CÆSAR. A famous Roman who, after the battle of Actium, had bestowed on him by the senate the surname *Augustus*, as expressing his dignity and greatness. See Augustus.

ODENA'TUS. A celebrated prince of Palmyra. At an early period of his life he inured himself to bear fatigue by hunting wild beasts. He was a faithful ally of the Romans, and gave great offence to Sapor, king of Persia, in consequence. In the warfare which ensued he obtained advantage over the troops of Sapor, and took his wife prisoner, besides gaining great booty. He died by the hand of one of his relations whom he had offended. Zenobia succeeded him on the throne.

O'DIN. In Scandinavian mythology the god of the universe, and reputed father of all the Scandinavian kings. His wife's name was Friga, and his two sons were Thor and Balder.

ODYS'SEUS. See Ulysses.

ŒDIPUS. A son of Laius, king of Thebes, and Jocasta. Laius was informed by the oracle, as soon as he married Jocasta, that he would perish by the hands of his son. On his birth Œdipus was given to a domestic, with orders to expose him to death on the mountains, where he was found by one of the shepherds of Polybus, king of Corinth. Peribœa, wife of Polybus, educated him as her own child, tending him with great care. In after life he met Laius in a narrow lane in a chariot, and being haughtily ordered to make way for Laius, a combat ensued in which Laius was slain. After this Œdipus was attracted to Thebes by the fame of the Sphinx, who devoured all those who attempted to explain without success the enigmas which she propounded. The enigma proposed by the Sphinx to Œdipus was:—What animal in the morning walks upon four feet, at noon upon two, and in the evening upon three? Œdipus solved the riddle by replying that the animal was a man, who in childhood crawls on his hands and feet, on attaining manhood walks on two feet erect, and in the evening of life supports his tottering steps with a staff. The monster, on hearing the correct solution of the riddle, dashed her head against a rock and perished.

ŒNEUS. A king of Calydon, son of Parthaon or Portheus and Euryte. He married Althæa, their children being Clymenus, Meleager, Gorge, and Dejanira. In a general sacrifice he made to the gods he slighted Diana, who, in revenge, sent a wild boar to waste his country. The animal was killed by Meleager in the celebrated Calydonian boar hunt. After this misfortunes overtook Œneus, and he exiled himself from Calydon, and died on his way to Argolis.

ŒNOM'AUS. King of Pisa, in Elis, and father of Hippodamia, son of Mars. He was told by the oracle that he would perish by his son-in-law. Being skilled in driving a chariot, he announced that he would give his daughter in marriage only to some one who could defeat him in a race, death being the result to those who were defeated. After a number of aspirants had contended and failed, Pelops, son Tantalus, entered the lists, and by bribing the charioteer of Œnomaus, who provided a chariot with a broken axle-tree, Pelops won the race, and married Hippodamia, becoming king of Pisa. Œnomaus was killed in the race.

Œno'ne. A nymph of Mount Ida, who had the gift of prophecy; wife of Paris, who deserted her for Helen.

Ogyg'ia. An island, the abode of Calypso, in the Mediterranean Sea. It was so beautiful in sylvan scenery that even Mercury (who dwelt on Olympus) was charmed with the spot.

Ole'nus. A daughter of Vulcan, wife of Lethæa, a woman who thought herself more beautiful than the goddesses, and as a punishment she and her husband were turned into stone statues.

Olym'pia. Celebrated games which received their name either from Olympia, where they were observed, or from Jupiter Olympius, to whom they were dedicated. They were held every four years from the earliest times.

Olym'pus. A mountain in Macedonia and Thessaly. The ancients supposed that it touched the heavens, and thus they have made it the residence of the gods, and the place where Jupiter (Zeus) held his court. On the top of the mountain, according to the poets, eternal spring reigned.

Olym'pius. A name of Jupiter (Zeus), from Olympia, where the god had a splendid temple, which was considered to be one of the seven wonders of the world.

Om'phale. A queen of Lydia, daughter of Jardanus. She married Tmolus, who, at his death, left her mistress of his kingdom. She had heard of the exploits of Hercules, and wished to see him. After he had slain Eurytus, Hercules was ordered to be sold as a slave, and was purchased by Omphale, who gave him his liberty. He became in love with Omphale, who reciprocated his passion. He is represented by the poets as being so infatuated with her that he sat spinning by her side surrounded by her women, while she garbed herself with his lion's skin, arming herself with his club.

OPA'LIA. Roman festivals in honor of Ops, held on 14th of the calends of January.

OPPIA'NUS. A Greek poet of Cilicia. He wrote some poems celebrated for their sublimity and elegance. Caracalla gave him a piece of gold for every verse in one of his poems. Oppian died of the plague in the thirtieth year of his age.

OPS. A daughter of Cœlus and Terra, the same as the Rhea of the Greeks, who married Saturn, and became mother of Jupiter. She was known among the ancients by the different names of Cybele, Bona, Dea, Magna Mater, Thya, Tellus, and Proserpina. She was the Roman deity of plenty.

ORÆ'A. Certain sacrifices offered to the goddesses of the seasons to invoke fair weather for the ripening of the fruits of the earth.

ORBO'NA. The goddess of orphans.

ORES'TES. A son of Agamemnon and Clytemnestra. His father was slain by Clytemnestra and Ægisthus, but young Orestes was saved from his mother's dagger by his sister Electra, called by Homer Laodicea, and was conveyed to the house of Strophius, king of Phocis, who had married a sister of Agamemnon. He was indulgently treated by Strophius, who educated him with his son Pylades. The two young princes formed the most inviolable friendship. When Orestes had arrived at years of manhood he avenged his father's death by killing his mother Clytemnestra.

OR'IGEN. A Greek writer, celebrated for his learning and the sublimity of his genius. He suffered martyrdom in his sixty-ninth year. His works are numerous, consisting of commentaries on the Scriptures and various treatises. He died A. D. 253.

ORI'ON. A famous, handsome giant, who was blinded by Œnopion for a grievous wrong done to Merope, and he was expelled from Chios. The sound of the Cyclop's hammer led him to the abode of Vulcan (Hephæstus) who gave him a guide. He then consulted an oracle, and had his sight restored.

ORI′THY′IA. A daughter of Erechtheus, whose lover, Boreas, carried her off while she was wandering by the river Ilissus. Her children were Zetes and Calais, two winged warriors who accompanied the Argonauts.

OR′MUZD. In Persian mythology the creator of all things.

OR′PHEUS. A son of Œger and the Muse Calliope. Some suppose him to be the son of Apollo. He received a lyre from Apollo, or, according to some, from Mercury, on which he played in such a masterly manner that the melodious sounds caused rivers to cease to flow, and savage beasts to forget their wildness. He married Eurydice, who died from the bite of a serpent. Orpheus felt her death acutely, and to recover her he visited the infernal regions. Pluto, the king of the infernal regions, was enraptured with the strains of music from the lyre of Orpheus, and according to the poets, the wheel of Ixion stopped, the stone of Sisyphus stood still, Tantalus forgot his burning thirst, and even the Furies relented, so fascinating were the sounds extracted from the lyre. Pluto was moved by the sorrow of Orpheus, and consented to restore Eurydice to him, provided he forbore to look behind him till he had reached the extremity of his domain. Orpheus agreed to this, but forgot his promise, and turned round to look at Eurydice, who instantly vanished from his sight. After this he separated himself from the society of mankind, and the Thracian women, whom he had offended by his coldness, attacked him while they celebrated the orgies of Bacchus, and after they had torn his body to pieces they threw his head into the Hebrus.

OS′SA. One of the mountains which the giants piled on the top of Olympus to enable them to ascend to heaven and attack the gods.

OS′TIA. A town at the mouth of the river Tiber and the harbor of Rome. It was founded by Ancus Marcius, the fourth king of Rome.

OSI'RIS. A great deity of the Egyptians, husband of Isis. The ancients differ in opinion concerning this celebrated god, but they all agree that as ruler of Egypt he took care to civilize his subjects, to improve their morals, to give them good and salutary laws, and to teach them agriculture. In the Egyptian theogony he was the personation of all physical and moral good, and was styled Manifestor of Good, Lord of Lords, King of the Gods, etc. He fell a prey to the intrigues of his brother Set, the Typhon of the Greeks, who represented the sum of evil agencies, and then became judge of the dead. He is represented under many different forms, and compared sometimes to the sun and sometimes to the Nile. In particular his soul was supposed to animate a sacred bull called Apis, and thus to be continually present among men. See Apis.

Osiris.

OTH'O. Roman emperor from January 16 to April 16, A. D. 69. He committed suicide upon being defeated by Vitellius, who had been proclaimed emperor by the army.

OVID'IUS P. NA'SO, usually called OVID. A celebrated Roman poet, born at Sulmo. He was sent at an early age to Rome, and afterwards went to Athens in the sixteenth year of his age, where his progress in the study of eloquence was great. His natural inclination, however, was towards poetry, and to this he devoted his chief attention. His lively genius and fertile imagination soon gained him admirers; the learned became his friends; Virgil, Propertius, Horace, and Tibullus, honored him with their correspondence, and Augustus patronized him with unbounded liberality. These favors, however, were transitory, and he was banished to a place on the Euxine Sea by order of the emperor. The true cause of his banishment is not known. His friends ardently entreated the emperor to permit him to return, but in vain, and he died in the seventh or eighth year of his banishment, in the fifty-ninth year of his age, A. D. 17. A great portion of his works remains. These consist of the "Metamorphoses," "Fasti," "Epistolæ," etc. While his works are occasionally disfigured by indelicacy, they are distinguished by great sweetness and elegance.

Ox'us. A great river of Central Asia.

P

Pacto'lus. A celebrated river of Lydia. It was in this river that Midas washed himself when he turned into gold whatever he touched.

Pac'inrus, M. One of the early Roman tragic authors, born B. C. 220, and was the nephew of Ennius. He was also an artist.

Pæ'an. A surname of Apollo derived from the word *paean*, a hymn which was sung in his honor for killing the serpent Python.

Palæ'mon or Pale'mon. A sea deity, son of Athamas and Ino. His original name was Melicerta. He assumed the name of Palæmon after being changed into a sea deity by Neptune (Poseidon).

Palame'des. A Grecian chief, son of Nauplius, king of Eubœa, and Clymene. He was sent by the Greek princes, who were going to the Trojan war, to bring Ulysses to the camp, who, to withdraw himself from the expedition, had pretended to be insane. Palamedes soon penetrated the deception, and Ulysses was obliged to join in the war, but an inveterate enmity arose between the two, and by an unworthy artifice Ulysses procured the death of Palamedes. Palamedes is accredited with the invention of dice, backgammon, and other games.

Palati'nus, Mons. A celebrated hill, the largest of the seven hills on which Rome was built.

Pa'les. The goddess of shepherds and protectress of flocks; her festivals were called Palilia.

Palinu'rus. A skillful pilot of the ship of Æneas. He fell into the sea while asleep, and was exposed to the waves for three days, and on reaching the shore was murdered by the inhabitants of the place where he landed.

Palla'dium. A celebrated statue of Athena (Minerva). It represented the goddess as holding a spear in her right hand, and in her left a distaff and spindle. It fell down from heaven near the tent of Ilus as he was building the citadel of Ilium, while, according to others, it fell in Phrygia; another account says Dardanus received it as a present from his mother Electra; other accounts are given of its origin. It is generally agreed, however, that on the preservation of the statue the fate of Troy depended. This was known to the Greeks during the Trojan war, and they contrived to obtain possession of it. But some authors say that the true Palladium was not carried away by the Greeks, but only a statue which had been placed near it, and which bore some resemblance to it.

PAL'LAS. A name of Minerva. She is said to have received the name because she killed a noted giant bearing that name. The goddess of wisdom among the Greeks, subsequently identified with the Roman Minerva.

PALMY'RA. The capital of Palmyrene, a country on the eastern boundaries of Syria, now called Tadmor. It is famous as being the seat of government of the celebrated Queen Zenobia.

PAN. The god of shepherds, huntsmen, and the inhabitants of the country, He was the son of Mercury (Hermes) by Callisto. He was in appearance a monster; he had two small horns on his head, and his legs, thighs, tail, and feet were like those of the goat. The original seat of his worship was the solitudes of Arcadia, whence it gradually spread over the rest of Greece. He is represented also as fond of music, and of dancing with the forest nymphs, and as the inventor of the syrinx or shepherd's flute, hence termed *Pan's-pipes* or *Pandean pipes*. The Romans identified the Greek Pan with their own Italian god Inuus,

Pallas.

Pan.

and sometimes also with Faunus. He is generally seen playing a pipe made of reeds of various lengths, which he invented himself, and from which he could produce music which charmed even the gods. Pan's terrific appearance once so frightened the Gauls when they invaded Greece that they ran away though no one pursued them; and the word *panic* is said to have been derived from this episode. The Fauns, who greatly resembled Pan, were his attendants.

PAN'DARUS. A son of Lycaon, who aided the Trojans in their war with the Greeks. He broke the truce which had been agreed on by the contending armies, and wounded Menelaus and Diomedes. He was at last killed by Diomedes.

PANDI'ON. A king of Athens, father of Procne and Philomela. During his reign there was such an abundance of corn, wine, and oil in his realm, that it was supposed that Bacchus (Dionysus) and Ceres (Demeter) had personally visited the country.

PANDO'RA. A celebrated woman; the first mortal female that ever lived, according to Hesiod. She was made of clay by Vulcan (Hephæstus), and having received life, all the gods made presents to her. Venus (Aphrodite) gave her beauty and the art of pleasing; the Graces gave her the power of captivating; Apollo taught her how to sing, and Mercury (Hermes) instructed her in eloquence. Jupiter (Zeus) gave her a beautiful box, which she was ordered to present to the man who married her. This was Epimetheus, brother of Prometheus, who opened the box, from which issued a multitude of evils, which became dispersed all over the world, and which from that fatal moment have never ceased to affect the human race. Hope alone remained at the bottom of the box.

PAN'SA, C. VIB'IUS. A Roman consul, who, with Hirtius, pursued the assassins of Cæsar, and was killed in a battle near Mutina.

PAN'THEON. A celebrated temple at Rome, built by Agrippa in the reign of Augustus, and dedicated to all the gods. It was 144 feet in diameter, and 144 feet high; and was built in the Corinthian style of architecture, mostly of marble; while its walls were covered with engraved brass and silver.

PAP'HUS. Son of Pygmalion by the statue into which life had been breathed by Venus (Aphrodite). Pygmalion is sometimes called the Paphian hero.

PAR'CÆ. The Fates, powerful goddesses who presided over the birth and life of mankind. They were three in number, Clotho, Lachesis, and Atropos, daughters of Nox and Erubus, according to Hesiod, or, according to what he says in another place, of Jupiter and Themis.

PAR'IS. The son of Priam, king of Troy, and Hecuba; he was also called Alexander. He was destined before his birth to cause the ruin of his country, and before he was born his mother dreamed that he would be a torch which would set fire to her palace. The soothsayers predicted that he would be the cause of the destruction of Troy. In consequence of these foretold calamities Priam ordered a slave to destroy the child immediately after birth, but instead of acting thus the slave exposed the child on Mount Ida, where some shepherds found him and took care of him. Paris gave early proofs of courage, and his graceful countenance recommended him to Œnone, a nymph of Ida, whom he married. At the marriage of Peleus and Thetis, the goddess of discord who had not been invited, showed her displeasure by throwing into the assembly of the gods, who were at the nuptials, a golden apple, on which were the words:—Let it be given to the fairest. The apple was claimed by Juno (Hera), Venus (Aphrodite), and Minerva (Athena). Paris, who had been appointed to award it to the most beautiful of the three goddesses, gave it to Venus. Subsequently Paris visited Sparta, where he persuaded Helen, wife of Menelaus, the most beautiful woman of the age, to elope with him. This caused the Trojan war. Different accounts are given of the death of Paris. By some he is said to have been killed by one of the arrows of Philoctetes which had once belonged to Hercules.

PARME'NIO. A celebrated general in the armies of Alexander the Great, by whom he was regarded with the greatest affection. The firm friendship which existed between the two generals was broken in a sudden fit of anger by Alexander, who ordered his friend to be put to death, B. C. 330.

PARNAS'SUS. A mountain of Phocis, sacred to the Muses, and to Apollo and Bacchus (Dionysus). It was named thus after a son of Neptune (Poseidon) who bore that designation. It was sacred to Apollo and Bacchus. Any one who slept on this mountain became a poet. It was named after one of the sons of Bacchus.

PARRHA'SIUS. A famous painter of Ephesus in the age of Zeuxis, about 1,500 years before Christ. He contended on one occasion with Zeuxis for the palm in painting, and Zeuxis acknowledged that he was excelled by Parrhasius.

PAR'THENON. A temple of Athens sacred to Minerva (Pallas—Athena). It is considered the most beautiful building of antiquity. It stood on the hill called the Acropolis. The ruins are still standing. It was destroyed by the Persians, and was rebuilt by Pericles.

PASIPH'Æ. A daughter of the Sun (Helios) and of Perseis, who married Minos, king of Crete. She became the mother of the Minotaur, who was killed by Theseus.

PATRO'CLUS. One of the Grecian chiefs during the Trojan war. He contracted an intimate friendship with Achilles, and when the Greeks went to the Trojan war Patroclus accompanied them. He was the constant companion of Achilles, living in the same tent, and when his friend refused to appear on the field of battle, because of being offended with Agamemnon, Patroclus imitated his example. Nestor, however, prevailed on him again to take the field, and Achilles lent him his armor. Hector encountered him, and after a desperate fight slew him. The Greeks obtained his dead body, which was brought into the Grecian camp, where Achilles received it with great lamentation, and again taking the field, killed Hector, thus avenging the death of his friend.

PAU'LUS ÆMIL'IUS. A Roman celebrated for his military achievements, surnamed "Macedonicus" from his conquest of Macedonia. In early life he distinguished himself by his application and for his love for military discipline. In his first consulship he reduced the Ligurians to subjection, and subsequently obtained a great victory over the Macedonians, making himself master of the country. In the office of censor, which he filled, he behaved with great moderation, and at his death, about 168 B. C., the Romans mourned deeply for him.

PAUSA'NIAS. A Spartan general who greatly signalized himself at the battle of Platæa against the Persians. He afterwards, at the head of the Spartan armies, extended his conquests to Asia, but the haughtiness of his behavior made him many enemies. He offered, on certain conditions, to betray Greece to the Persians, but his perfidy was discovered, on which he fled for safety to a temple of Minerva (Athena), where he was starved to death, B. C. 471.

PA'VAN. The Hindoo god of the winds.

PEG'ASUS. A winged horse sprung from the blood of Medusa, when she was killed by Perseus. According to Ovid he fixed his abode on Mount Helicon, where, by striking the earth with his foot, he raised a fountain which has been called Hippocrene.

PELAS'GI, the earliest inhabitant of Greece. They are said to have been an agricultural people with some knowledge of the useful arts. The Athenians were supposed to be descended from them.

PE'LEUS. A king of Thessaly, son of Æacus and Endeis, the daughter of Chiron. He married Thetis, one of the Nereids.

PE'LIAS. Son of Neptune (Poseidon) and Tyro. On his birth he was exposed to the woods, but his life was preserved by some shepherds. Subsequently Tyro was married to Cretheus, king of Iolchos. They had three children, of whom Æson was the eldest. Pelias visited his mother after the death of Cretheus, and usurped the authority which properly belonged to the children of the deceased monarch. Jason, the son of Æson, who had been educated by Chiron, on attaining manhood demanded the kingdom, the government of which Pelias had usurped. Jason was persuaded by Pelias to waive his claim for the present, and start on the Argonautic expedition. On his return, accompanied by the sorceress Medea, she undertook to restore Pelias to youth, explaining that it was necessary first to cut his body to pieces and place the limbs in a caldron of boiling water. This was done, when Medea refused to fulfill her promise, which she had solemnly made to the daughters of Pelias, who were four in number, and who had received the patronymic of the "Peliades."

PE'LION, sometimes called Pellos. A celebrated mountain of Thessaly, the top of which is covered with pine trees, and famous for the wars between the giants and the gods, and as the abode of the Centaurs, who were expelled by the Lapithæ.

PELOP'IDAS. A celebrated general of Thebes, son of Hippoclus. It was owing to his valor and prudence, combined with the ability of Epaminondas, that the famous victory of Leuctra was won; B. C. 371.

PELLOPONNE'SUS. The southern part of Greece, or the peninsula which was connected with Greece proper by the isthmus of Corinth. Its principal provinces were Achaia, Arcadia, Laconia and Corinthia.

PE'LOPS. A celebrated prince, son of Tantalus, king of Phrygia. He was killed by his father, and served up as a feast to the gods, who had visited Phrygia. He was restored to life, and married Hippodamia, having won her through defeating her father in a chariot race.

PENA'TES. Certain inferior deities among the Romans, who presided over the domestic affairs of families.

PENEL'OPE. A celebrated princess of Greece, daughter of Icarius, and wife of Ulysses, king of Ithaca. She became the mother of Telemachus, and was obliged to part, with great reluctance, from her husband when the Greeks obliged him to go to the Trojan war. The strife between the hostile forces continued for ten years, and when Ulysses did not return home at the conclusion of the war her fears and anxieties became overwhelming. She was beset by a number of suitors, who told her that her husband would never return, and she ought to give herself to one of her admirers. She received their advances with coldness, but as she was devoid of power, and, as it were, almost a prisoner in their hands, she temporized with them. After twenty years' absence Ulysses returned, and at once delivered her from the persecutions of her suitors. The accounts given by different authors respecting her, in fact, differ materially. By some she is said to have been the mother of Pan.

PENTHESILE'A. A queen of the Amazons, daughter of Mars (Ares). She came to assist Priam in the last years of the Trojan war, and was slain by Achilles.

PER'DIX, the sister of Daedalus, or, according to some, the nephew of Daedalus. Said to be the inventor of the chisel, the compasses, and the potter's wheel. His skill excited the jealousy of Daedalus, who threw him from a temple of Athena (Minerva), but the goddess changed him into a bird, the partridge.

PER'GAMUS. The citadel of the city of Troy. The word is often used to signify Troy. From it Xerxes reviewed his troops as he marched to invade Greece.

PER'ICLES. An Athenian of noble family, son of Xanthippus and Agariste. His naturally great mental powers were greatly improved by attending the lectures of Zeno and other philosophers. He became a commander, a statesman, and an orator, and gained the esteem of the people by his address and liberality. In his ministerial capacity, Pericles did not enrich himself. The prosperity and happiness of Athens was his primary object. He made war against the Lacedæmonians, and restored the temple of Delphi to the care of the Phocians, who had been improperly deprived of that honorable trust. The Peloponnesian war was fomented by his ambitious views. He at length lost his popularity, but only temporarily, and he was restored to all the honors of which he had been deprived. A pestilence which prevailed proved fatal to him in his seventieth year, about 429 B. C.

PERSE'PHONE, called Proserpina by the Romans. The daughter of Zeus (Jupiter) and Demeter (Ceres). She is the all pervading goddess of Nature, who produces and destroys everything.

PER'SEUS. A son of Jupiter (Zeus) and Danae, the daughter of Acrisius. It had been predicted by the oracle that Acrisius was to perish by his daughter's offspring, so Perseus, soon after his birth, was, with his mother Danae, thrown into the sea. Both were saved, and reached the island of Seriphos, where they were treated kindly by Polydectes, the king, who, however, soon became jealous of the genius of Perseus. Perseus had promised Polydectes to bring him the head of the Gorgon Medusa. To enable him to do this Pluto left him a helmet which made the wearer invisible, Minerva (Athena) gave him her buckler, and Mercury (Hermes) furnished him with wings. Thus equipped he found the Gorgons, and cut off Medusa's head, with which he fled through the air, and from the blood which dropped from it sprang the horse Pegasus. During his flight Perseus discovered Andromeda chained to a rock to be devoured by a sea monster, which he destroyed, and married Andromeda. He now returned to Seriphos, where he turned into stone Polydectes by showing him Medusa's head. By an accident, in throwing a quoit he killed Acrisius, thus fulfilling the prediction of the oracle.

PER'SEUS or PER'SES. A son of Philip, king of Macedonia. He distinguished himself by his enmity to the Romans, and when he had made sufficient preparations he declared war against them. He, however, wanted courage and resolution, and though he at first obtained some advantages over the Roman armies, his timidity proved destructive to his cause. He was defeated at Pydna, and soon after was taken prisoner, and died in prison at Rome.

PER'SIUS, AU'LUS FLAC'CUS. A Latin poet of Volaterræ. He was of a good family, and soon became intimate with the most illustrious Romans of his day. The early part of his life was spent in his native town, but at the age of sixteen he was removed to Rome, where he studied philosophy. He died in his thirtieth year, A. D. 62. The satires of Persius were read with pleasure and avidity by his contemporaries.

PER'TINAX, PUB'LIUS HEL'VIUS. A Roman emperor after the death of Commodus. He was descended from an obscure family, and for some time was employed in drying wood and making charcoal. He entered on a military life, and by his valor rose to offices of the highest trust, and was made consul. At the death of Commodus he was selected to succeed to the throne. His patriotism gained him the affection of the worthiest of his subjects, but there were some who plotted against him. He was killed by his soldier, A. D. 193.

PETRO'NIUS AR'BITER. A favorite of the emperor Nero, and one of the ministers and associates of his pleasures and vices. He was made proconsul of Bithynia, and afterwards was honored with the consulship. Eventually he became out of favor with Nero, and resolved to des'roy himself, which he did by having his veins opened, A. D. 66. Petronius distinguished himself by his writings as well as by his voluptuousness. He is the author of many elegant compositions, which are, however, often characterized by impropriety of language.

PHÆ'DRA. A daughter of Minos and Pasiphæ, who married Theseus. She became the mother of Acamas and Demophoon. She brought an unjust accusation against Hippolytus (a son of Theseus before she married him), who was killed by the horses in his chariot taking fright, causing him to be thrown under the wheels and crushed to death. On hearing this Phædra acknowledged the falseness of the charge she had brought against Hippolytus, and hanged herself in despair.

PHÆ'DRUS. A Thracian who became one of the freedmen of the emperor Augustus. He translated the fables of Æsop into Iambic verse.

PHA'ETHON. A son of the Sun, or of Phœbus and Clymene. According to Hesiod and Pausanias he was the son of Cephalus and Aurora, or of Tithonus and Aurora according to Apollodorus. He is, however, generally acknowledged to be the son of Phœbus and Clymene. Phœbus allowed him to drive the chariot of the Sun for one day. Phaethon, on receiving the reins, at once showed his incapacity; the horses became unmanageable, and heaven and earth were threatened with a conflagration, when Jupiter struck Phaethon with a thunderbolt, and hurled him in the river Po, where he perished.

PHAL'ARIS. A tyrant of Agrigentum, who treated his subjects with great cruelty. Perillus made him a brazen bull, inside of which he proposed to place culprits, and by applying fire burn them to death. The first to be thus burnt in this manner was Perillus himself. The cruelties practiced by Phalaris were revenged by a revolt of his people, who put him to death by burning him in the bull.

PHALER'UM. One of the harbors of Athens.

PHA'ON. A boatman of Mitylene, in Lesbos. He received a box of ointment from Venus (Aphrodite), who had presented herself to him in the form of an old woman. When he had rubbed himself with the unguent he became beautiful, and Sappho, the celebrated poetess, became enamored of him. For a short time he devoted himself to her, but soon treated her with coldness, upon which she threw herself into the sea and was drowned.

PHARNABA'ZUS. A satrap of Persia who assisted the Lacedæmonians against the Athenians, and gained their esteem by his devotion to their cause.

PHA'ROS. A small island in the bay of Alexandria, on which was built a tower for a lighthouse which was considered one of the seven wonders of the world. It was erected in the reigns of Ptolemy Soter and Ptolemy Philadelphus, the architect being Sostratus, the son of Dexiphanes.

PHARSA'LIA. A town of Thessaly, famous for the great battle fought there between Julius Cæsar and Pompey, in which the former obtained the victory.

PHID'IAS. A celebrated sculptor of Athens, who died B. C. 432. He executed a statue of Minerva (Athena), which was placed in the Pantheon. He was the greatest sculptor of antiquity.

PHIL'ADELPHIE. A city of Asia Minor east of the Jordan.

PHIL'EMON. A Greek writer of comedies who flourished about B. C. 330.

PHILIP'PI. A town of Macedonia, celebrated for two battles fought there, B. C. 42, between Augustus and Antony and the republican forces of Brutus and Cassius, in which the former were victorious.

PHILIP'PUS, king of Macedonia, was son of Amyntas, king of Macedonia. He learned the art of war from Epaminondas. He married Olympias, the daughter of Neoptolemus, king of the Molossi, and became father of Alexander the Great. Among the most important events of his reign was the battle of Chæronea, which he won from the Greeks. The character of Philip is that of a sagacious, prudent, but artful and intriguing monarch. He was assassinated by Pausanias at the celebration of the nuptials of his daughter, in the forty-seventh year of his age and the twenty-fourth of his reign, about 336 years before the Christian era.

PHILIP'PUS. The last king of Macedonia of that name was son of Demetrius. He aspired to become the friend of Hannibal. His intrigues were discovered by the Romans, who invaded his territories, and extorted peace from him on terms which were humiliating. He died in the forty-second year of his reign, 179 years before the Christian era.

PHI'LO. A Jewish writer of Alexandria, A. D. 40. His works related to the creation of the world, sacred history, and the laws and customs of the Jewish nation.

PHILOCTE'TES was one of the Argonauts. He received from Hercules the arrows which he had dipped in the gall of the Hydra. The Greeks, in the tenth year of the Trojan war, were informed by the oracle that Troy could not be taken without these arrows. Philoctetes repaired to the Grecian camp, where he destroyed a number of the Trojans, among whom was Paris, with the arrows. The adventures of Philoctetes are the subject of one of the best tragedies of Sophocles.

PHILOME'LA. A daughter of Pandion, king of Athens. Her sister Procne had married Tereus, king of Thrace, and being separated from Philomela, spent her time in great melancholy. She persuaded her husband to go to Athens and bring her sister to Thrace. Tereus, on the journey, treated Philomela with great cruelty, and cut off her tongue, confining her in a lonely castle, and reporting to Procne that she was dead. Philomela, however, found means to inform Procne that she was living. In revenge for the cruelty of Tereus, Procne murdered his son and served him up as food at a banquet. On hearing this Tereus drew his sword to slay the sisters, when he was changed into a hoopoe, Philomela into a nightingale, and

Procne into a swallow. In poetry we frequently find the nightingale alluded to as Philomela.

PHILOPOE'MEN. A celebrated general of the Achæans, born at Megalopolis. At an early age he distinguished himself on the field of battle, at the same time appearing fond of agriculture and a country life. He adopted Epaminondas as his model, and was not unsuccessful in imitating the prudence and other good qualities of the famous Theban. When Megalopolis was attracted by the Spartans, Philopoemen, then in his thirtieth year, gave the most decisive proofs of his valor. Raised to the rank of commander, he showed his ability to discharge that important trust, by killing with his own hand Mechanidas, the tyrant of Sparta, and defeating his army. Sparta having become, after its conquest, tributary to the Achæans, Philopoemen enjoyed the triumph of having subdued one of the most powerful states of Greece. He was at length made prisoner by the Messenians, and was treated by their general, Dinocrates, with great severity. He was poisoned in his seventieth year, about 183 years B. C.

PHILOS'TRATUS. A famous Sophist born at Lemnos, or, according to some, at Athens. He came to Rome, where he was patronized by Julia, the wife of the emperor Severus. She entrusted him with some papers referring to Apollonius, whose life he wrote. This biography was written with elegance, but contains many exagerated descriptions and improbable stories He lived about 244 A. D.

PHI'NEUS. A son of Agenor, king of Phœnicia, or, according to some, a son of Neptune (Poseidon), who became king of Thrace. He married Cleopatra (called by some Cleobula), the daughter of Boreas, their children being Plexippus and Pandion. After the death of Cleopatra, he married Idæa, the daughter of Dardanus, who, jealous of Cleopatra's children, accused them of an attempt on their father's life, and they were condemned by Phineus to have their eyes put out. This cruelty was punished by the gods, Phineus being made blind, and the Harpies were sent by Jupiter to keep him in continual alarm. He recovered his sight by means of the Argonauts, whom he received with great hospitality.

PHLEG'ETHON. A river in the infernal regions, between the banks of which flames of fire flowed instead of water.

PHLE'GON. One of the emperor Adrian's freedmen. He wrote a historical account of Sicily, an account of the principal places in Rome, and treatises on different subjects. His style was inelegant, and he evinced a want of judgment in his writings.

PHLE'GYAS. Son of Mars and father of Ixion and Coronis. For his impiety in desecrating and plundering the temple of Apollo at Delphi, he was sent to Hades, and there was made to sit with a huge stone suspended over his head, ready to be dropped on him at any moment.

PHŒ'BUS. A name of Apollo, signifying light and life.

PHO'CION. An Athenian celebrated for his public and private virtues. He was distinguished for his zeal for the general good, and for his military abilities. The fickleness of the Athenians, however, caused them to lose sight of his virtues, and being accused of treason, he was condemned to drink poison, which he took with the greatest heroism. His death occurred about 318 years B. C.

PHO'CIS. A district in northern Greece.

PHŒ'NICE or PHŒ'NICIA. A country of Asia, on the coast of the Mediterranean. A great maritime nation that planted colonies all over the shores of Africa and Southern Europe. Carthage was originally a Phœnician colony.

PHŒ'NIX. Son of Amyntor, king of Argos, and Cleobule or Hippodamia, was preceptor to Achilles. He accompanied his pupil to the Trojan war, and Achilles was ever grateful for the precepts he had received from him. After the fall of Troy he died in Thrace, and, according to Strabo, was buried near Trachinia, where his name was given to a river.

PHRYG'IA. A country of Asia Minor.

PHRY'NE. A beautiful woman who lived at Athens about 328 years before the Christian era. She was beloved by Praxiteles, who painted her portrait. It is said that Apelles painted his Venus Anadyomene after he had seen

Phryne on the seashore with dishevelled hair. There was another woman of the same name, who was accused of impiety. When her judges were about to condemn her she unveiled her bosom, and her beauty so captivated them that they acquitted her.

PHRYX'US. A son of Athamas, king of Thebes, and Nephele. On the plea of insanity, Nephele was repudiated by Athamas, who then married Ino, who persecuted Phryxus with inveterate hatred, because he was to succeed to the throne in preference to one of her own children. Being apprised that Ino had designs on his life, he started with his sister Helle to go to Ætes, king of Colchis. According to the poets they mounted on a ram, whose fleece was gold, which soared into the air, directing its course to Colchis. Helle became giddy, and falling into the sea (afterwards called the Hellespont), was drowned. Phryxus arrived at the court of Ætes, whose daughter Chalciope he married. Some time afterwards he was killed by his father-in-law. The murder of Phryxus gave rise to the famous Argonautic expedition under Jason, the object being to recover the Golden Fleece, which Jason succeeded in obtaining.

PHYL'LIS. A daughter of Sithon, or, according to other writers, of Lycurgus, king of Thrace. She received Demophoon, who landed on her coasts on his return from the Trojan war, and fell in love with him, and he reciprocated her affection; but afterwards proving faithless, Phyllis hanged herself, and according to an old tradition, was changed into an almond tree.

PIC'TOR FABI'US. The earliest Roman painter, flourished B. C. 307.

PICUM'NUS. A rural divinity, who presided over the manuring of lands, called also Sterentius.

PI'CUS. King of Latium, son of Saturn, who married Venilla. As he was hunting he was met by Circe, who became enamored with him. She changed him into a woodpecker.

PIER'IDES. A name given to the muses, because they were born in Pieria, or, as some say, because they were supposed to be the daughters of Pierus, a king of Macedonia, who settled in Bœotia.

PILUM'NUS. A rural divinity, which presided over the corn while it was being ground.

PIN'DARUS. A celebrated lyric poet of Thebes. When he was young it is said that a swarm of bees settled on his lips and left on them some honey, which was regarded as a sign of his future greatness. After his death great respect was shown to his memory, and a statue was erected in his honor in one of the most public places in Thebes. Pindar is said to have died at the age of eighty-six, B. C. 435. Of his works, the odes only are extant; they are admired for sublimity of sentiment and grandeur of expression.

PIRÆ'US. A celebrated harbor at Athens, about three miles from the city. It was joined to the town by two walls, one built by Pericles, and the other by Themistocles.

PIRITH'OUS. Son of Ixion and Dia, the daughter of Deioneus. He was king of the Lapithæ, and wished to become acquainted with Theseus, king of Athens, of whose fame and exploits he had heard. They became cordial friends. Pirithous married Hippodamia, and invited the Centaurs to attend his nuptials, where, having become intoxicated, they behaved with great rudeness, on which they were attacked and over come by Theseus, Pirithous, Hercules, and the rest of the Lapithæ. Many of the Centaurs were slain, and the rest saved their lives by flight.

PISAN'DER. A commander in the Spartan fleet during the Peloponnesian war. He was greatly opposed to democracy at Athens. He was killed in a naval battle near Cnidus, B. C. 394.

PISIS'TRATUS. A celebrated Athenian who distinguished himself by valor on the field and by eloquence at home. He obtained a bodyguard of fifty men to defend his person, and having thus got a number of armed men on whom he could rely, he seized the citadel of Athens, and soon made himself absolute. After this a conspiracy was formed against him, and he was banished from the city. He soon however, re-established himself in power, and married the daughter of Megacles, one of his greatest enemies, whom he afterwards repudiated. On this his popularity waned, and he fled from Athens, but after an absence of eleven years he returned, and was received by the people with acclamation. He died about 527 years B. C.

Pi'so. A celebrated family at Rome, eleven of whom had obtained the consulship, and some of whom had been honored with triumphs for their victories. Of this family the most famous were—LUCIUS CALPURNIUS, who was tribune of the people about 149 years B. C. and afterwards consul. He gained honor as an orator, a statesman, and a historian. CAIUS, another of the family, distinguished himself during his consulship by his firmness in resisting the tumults raised by the tribunes and the clamors of the people. CNEIUS, who was consul under Augustus, rendered himself odious by his cruelty. He was accused of poisoning Germanicus, and, being shunned by his friends, destroyed himself. LUCIUS, a governor of Spain, who was assassinated by a peasant. LUCIUS, a governor of Rome for twenty years, during which time he discharged his duties with moderation and justice. CAIUS, who was at the head of a conspiracy against Nero committed suicide by venesection.

PIT'TACUS, a native of Mitylene in Lesbos, was one of the seven wise men of Greece. He died in the eighty-second year of his age, about 570 years B. C. the latter part of his life being spent in retirement. Many of his maxims were inscribed on the walls of Apollo's temple at Delphi, to show how high an opinion his countrymen entertained of his abilities as a moralist and philosopher.

PLAN'CUS, L. MUNA'TIUS. A Roman conspicuous for his follies and extravagance. He had been consul, and had presided over a province, but he forgot his dignity, and became one of the most servile flatterers of Antony and Cleopatra.

PLATÆ'A. A town of Bœotia, near Mount Citheron, celebrated as the scene of a battle between Mardonius, the general of Xerxes, king of Persia, and Pausanias, who commanded the Athenians. The Persians were defeated with great slaughter.

PLA'TO. A celebrated philosopher of Athens. He was educated carefully, his mind being cultivated by the study of poetry and geometry, while his body was invigorated by the practice of gymnastics. He began his literary career by writing poetry and tragedies. At the age of twenty he was introduced to Socrates, with whom he was for some time a pupil. After travelling in various countries, he retired to the neighborhood of Athens, where his lectures were attended by a crowd of learned, noble, and illustrious pupils. He died on his birthday in the eighty-first year of his age, about 348 years B. C. His writings were so celebrated, and his opinions so highly regarded, that he was called the Divine.

PLAU'TUS, M. AC'CIUS, a Latin dramatic poet born in Umbria. He wrote twenty-five comedies, of which only nineteen are extant. He died about 184 years B. C. He was the greatest of the Latin comedians.

PLEI'ADES. A name given to seven daughter of Atlas and Pleione. They were placed after death in the heavens, and formed a constellation.

PLIN'IUS, C. SECUN'DUS, called the Elder, was born at Verona, of a noble family. He distinguished himself in the field, and was appointed governor of Spain. When at Misenum in command of the Roman fleet, Pliny observed the appearence of a cloud of dust and ashes, which was the commencement of the famous eruption of Mount Vesuvius which overwhelmed Herculaneum and Pompeii. He sailed for the scene of the eruption, where he was suffocated by the vapors emitted. This occured in the seventy-ninth year of the Christian era.

PLIN'IUS, C. CÆCIL'IUS SECUN'DUS, surnamed the Younger Pliny, was son of L. Cæcilius by the sister of Pliny the Elder. At the age of nineteen he distinguished himself at the bar. When Trajan was invested with the purple, Pliny was created consul. He died in the fifty-second year of his age, A. D. 113. Pliny had much to do with the persecutions of the Christians in the early promulgation of the Christian religion.

PLUTAR'CHUS, the celebrated biographer, was born at Chæronea, his father being distinguished for his learning and virtues. After traveling in quest of knowledge, he retired to Rome, where he opened a school. Subsequently he removed to Chæronea, where he died at an advanced age about A. D. 140. His most celebrated work is the Lives of Illustrious Men.

PLU'TO, son of Saturn and Ops, inherited his father's kingdom with his brothers, Jupiter (Zeus) and Neptune (Poseidon). He received as his portion the kingdom of the infernal regions, of death, and funerals. He seized Proserpina as she was gathering flowers, and carrying her away on his chariot, she became his wife and queen of the infernal regions. He is represented as an old man with a dignified but severe aspect, holding in his hand a two-pronged fork. He was generally called by the Greeks *Hades*, and by the Romans *Orcus*, *Tartarus*, and *Dis*.

Pluto and Proserpina.

PLU'TUS, the god of riches, was son of Jason and Ceres (Demeter). He is described as being blind and lame; blind because he so often injudiciously bestows his riches, and lame because fortunes come so slowly.

PLU'VIUS. A name of Jupiter among the Romans because he had the rain in his control.

PODALIR'IUS. A famous surgeon, a son of Æsculapius, who was very serviceable among the soldiers in the Trojan war.

POL'EMON. An eminent philosopher of Athens, a disciple of Plato. In his youth he was a profligate, but one day when passing the school of Xenocrates his attention was arrested by the lecture, and he remained an attentive listener. From that day he adopted an abstemious life, and devoted himself to philosophy. He died 273 B. C.

POL'LIO, C. ASIN'IUS. A Roman consul in the reign of Augustus, who distinguished himself equally by his eloquence and exploits in war. He wrote a history and some tragedies, and died in his eightieth year, A. D. 4.

POL'LUX. A son of Jupiter (Zeus) and Leda, brother to Castor.

POLYB'IUS. A native of Megalopolis in Arcadia. He distinguished himself by his valor against the Romans in Macedonia. He wrote an universal history in Greek, and died about 124 years B. C. His history consisted of 40 books.

POLYDEC'TES. A son of Magnes, king of Seriphos. He received with kindness Danae and her son Perseus, who had been exposed on the sea. Polydectes was turned into stone by being shown Medusa's head by Perseus.

POLYHYM'NIA. One of the Muses, daughter of Jupiter (Zeus) and Mnemosyne. She presided over singing and rhetoric.

POLYNI'CES. A son of Œdipus, king of Thebes, and Jocasta. He inherited his father's throne with his brother Eteocles, and it was agreed that they should reign a year alternately. Eteocles first ascended the throne, but refused to resign the crown. Polynices upon this fled to Argos, where he married Argia, the daughter of Adrastus, the king of the country, and levied an army with which he marched on Thebes. The battle was decided by a combat between the brothers, who killed each other.

POLYPHE'MUS. A celebrated Cyclops, son of Neptune (Poseidon) and Thoosa, the daughter of Phorcys. He is represented as a monster with one eye in the middle of his forehead. Ulysses was his captive, but escaped by putting a fire-brand in the monster's eye.

POMO'NA. A nymph at Rome, who was supposed to preside over the gardens and to be the goddess of fruit trees.

POMPE'II, or POMPEI'UM. A town of Campania. It was partly destroyed by an earthquake A. D. 63, and sixteen years afterwards it was swallowed up by an eruption of Mount Vesuvius. Herculaneum, in its vicinity, shared the same fate.

POMPE'IUS, CNEI'US, surnamed "the great," from his exploits, was son of Pompeius Strabo and Lucilia. In the contentions which existed between Marius and Sulla, Pompey linked himself with the latter. Subsequently he united his interest with that of Cæsar and Crassus, thus forming the first triumvirate. A breach soon occurred, and at the great battle of Pharsalia, where the forces of Cæsar and Pompey met, the latter was totally defeated, and fled to Egypt, where he was assassinated in the fifty-eighth year of his age, B. C. 48. He left two sons, Cneius and Sextus, who at their father's death were masters of a powerful army with which they opposed Cæsar, but were defeated at the battle of Munda, where Cneius was slain. Sextus escaped, and was put to death by Antony about 35 years B. C.

PONT'US. A district in the northeastern part of Asia Minor.

PONT'US EUX'MUS was the sea that is now called the Black Sea.

POR'CIA. A daughter of Cato of Utica, who married Bibulus, and after his death, Brutus. She was distinguished for her prudence and courage. After her husband's death she killed herself by swallowing burning coals. She is said to have given herself a severe wound to show that she could bear pain.

PORPHYR'IUS. A Platonic philosopher of Tyre. He studied eloquence at Athens under Longinus, and afterwards retired to Rome. His most celebrated work was in reference to the Christian religion. Porphyry died A. D. 304, aged seventy-one years.

PORSEN'NA or POR'SENA. A king of Etruria, who declared war against the Romans because they refused to restore Tarquin to the throne. He was prevented from entering the gates of Rome by the valor of P. Horatius Cocles, who at the head of a bridge kept back Porsenna's army, while the bridge was being cut down by the Romans to prevent the entry of their enemies into the city. Eventually Porsenna abandoned the cause of Tarquin. Macaulay, in his fine poem "Horatius," represents two other heroes, "Spurius Lartius" and "Herminius," as keeping the bridge on either hand of Horatius Cocles.

POSEI'DON, called Neptunus by the Romans. He was the god of the Mediterranean Sea, a son of Cronos (Saturn) and Rhea. He was a brother of Zeus (Jupiter), Hades (Pluto), Hera (Juno), and Demeter (Ceres).

PRÆN'ESTE. An ancient town of Latium.

PRAXIT'ELES. A famous sculptor of Greece, who lived about 324 B. C. The most famous of his works was a Cupid, which he gave to Phryne. He executed a statue of Phryne, and also one of Venus.

PRIAM'US. The last king of Troy; was the son of Laomedon, by Strymo, called Placia by some writers. He married Arisba, whom he divorced in order to marry Hecuba, by whom he had a number of children, the most celebrated of whom were Hector, Paris, Delphobus, Helenus, Laodice, and Cassandra. After he had reigned some time, Priam was anxious to recover his sister Hesione, who had been carried into Greece by Hercules, and to achieve this, he manned a fleet, the command of which he gave to his son Paris, who, instead of obeying the paternal instructions, carried away Helen, the wife of Menelaus, king of Sparta. This caused the Trojan war, which lasted for ten years. At the end of the war Priam was slain by Neoptolemus, the son of Achilles.

PRIA'PUS. The guardian of gardens and god of natural reproduction, was son of Venus (Aphrodite) and Bacchus (Dionysus).

PRO'BUS, M. AURE'LIUS. A native of Pannonia. His father was a gardener, who became a military tribune of Rome. His son obtained the same office on the twenty-second year of his age, and distinguished himself so much by his probity and valor that he was invested with the imperial purple. He encouraged the arts, and by his victories added to the glory of his country. He was slain by his soldiers in the fiftieth year of his age, B. C. 282.

PROCO'PIUS. Born of a noble family in Cilicia, was related to the emperor Julian. He signalized himself under Julian, and afterwards retired to the Thracian Chersonesus, whence he made his appearance at Constantinople, and proclaimed himself master of the Eastern Empire. He was defeated in Phrygia, and beheaded A. D. 366. There was a famous Greek historian of the same name, who wrote the history of the reign of Justinian, and who was secretary to Belisarius.

PROME'THEUS. A son of Iapetus and Clymene, one of the Oceanides. He ridiculed the gods and deceived Jupiter

(Zeus) himself, who, to punish him and the rest of mankind, took fire away from the earth; but Prometheus climbed the heavens by the assistance of Minerva (Athena), and stole fire from the chariot of the sun, which he brought down to the earth. This provoked Jupiter, and he ordered Prometheus to be chained to a rock, where a vulture was to feed on his liver, which was never exhausted. He was delivered from his tortures by Hercules, who killed the vulture.

PROPER'TIUS, SEX'TUS AURE'LIUS. A Latin poet born in Umbria. He came to Rome, where his genius greatly recommended him to the great and powerful. His works consist of four books of elegies which are marked by much ability. He died about 19 B. C.

PROSER'PINA. A daughter of Ceres (Demeter) and Jupiter (Zeus), called by the Greeks Persephone. As she was gathering flowers Pluto carried her off to the infernal regions, where he married her. Ceres, having learned that her daughter had been carried away by Pluto, demanded of Jupiter that Pluto should be punished. As queen of hell, Proserpina presided over the death of mankind. She was known by the name of Hecate, Juno Inferna, Libitina, and several others.

PROTAGORAS. A Greek philosopher of Abdera in Thrace. He wrote a book in which he denied the existence of a Supreme Being, which book was publicly burnt at Athens, and its author was banished from the city. He died B. C. 411.

PRO'TESILA'US. A king of part of Thessaly, who married Laodamia, and shortly afterwards went to the Trojan war. He was the first of the Greeks who entered the Trojan domain, and on that account, in accordance with the prediction of the oracle, was killed by his countrymen.

PRO'TEUS. A sea deity, son of Oceanus and Tethys, or, according to some writers, of Neptune (Poseidon) and Phenice. He had received the gift of prophecy from Neptune, but when consulted he often refused to give answers, and puzzled those who consulted him by assuming different shapes.

Psy'che. A nymph who married Cupid. A sort of mythical or allegorical personification of the human soul, a beautiful maiden, whose charming story is given by the Latin writer Appuleius. She was so beautiful as to be taken for Venus herself. This goddess, becoming jealous of her rival charms, ordered Cupid or Love to inspire her with love for some contemptible wretch. But Cupid fell in love with her himself. Many were the trials Psyche underwent, arising partly from her own indiscretion and partly from the hatred of Venus, with whom, however, a reconciliation was ultimately effected. Psyche by Jupiter's command, became immortal, and was for ever united with her beloved.

Cupid and Psyche—Antique.

Ptolemæ'us First, called Ptolemy, surnamed Lagus. A king of Egypt, son of Arsinoe and Lagus. He was educated in the court of the king of Macedonia, and when Alexander invaded Asia Ptolemy attended him. After Alexander's death Ptolemy obtained the government of Egypt, where he gained the esteem of the people by acts of kindness. He made himself master of Phœnica and Syria, and rendered assistance to the people of Rhodes against their enemies, for which he received the name of *Soter*. He laid the foundation of a library, which became the most celebrated in the world. He died in his eighty-fourth year, about 284 B. C. He was succeeded by his son Ptolemy Philadelphus, who showed himself to be a worthy successor of his father. His palace was an asylum for learned men, and he greatly increased the library his father had founded. Ptolemy Third succeeded his father Philadelphus on the Egyptian throne. He conquered Syria and Cilicia, and returned home laden with spoils. He was, like his predecessors, a patron of learning and the arts. Ptolemy Fourth, called Philopater, succeeded to the throne, his reign being marked by acts of cruelty and oppression. He died in his thirty-seventh year, after a reign of seventeen years, 204 years B. C. Numerous members of this celebrated family in succession occupied the throne, not, however, approaching to the greatness of the founders of the family.

PTOLEMÆ'US. A celebrated geographer and astronomer in the reign of Adrian and Antoninus. He was a native of Alexandria, or, as some say, of Pelusium. In his system of the world, designated the Ptolemaic system, he places the earth in the center of the universe, which was generally received as correct till it was confuted by Copernicus.

PUBLIC'OLA. A surname, signifying a friend of the common people, acquired by Publius Valerius. He assisted Brutus to expel the Tarquins from Rome, and won the victory in the battle in which Brutus and the sons of Tarquin had fallen. He was four times consul, but died in poverty, and was buried at the public expense amid general mourning.

PUD'ICITIA. A personification of modesty, worshipped at both Greece and Rome.

PYGMA'LION. A famous sculptor who had resolved to remain unmarried, but he made such a beautiful statue of a goddess that he begged Venus (Aphrodite) to give it life. His request being granted, Pygmalion married the animated statue.

PY'LOS. The name of three towns in the northern part of Greece.

PYR'RHUS. A famous king of Epirus, son of Æacides and Phthia. He wrote several books on encampments and the ways of training an army. He fought against the Romans with much valor, and they passed enconiums on his great military skill. He was killed in an attack on Argos, by a tile thrown on his head from a housetop.

PYTHAG'ORAS. A celebrated Greek philosopher born at Samos. He first made himself known in Greece at the Olympic games, where, when he was eighteen years old, he obtained the prize for wrestling. He also distinguished himself by his discoveries in geometry, astronomy, and mathematics. He was the first who supported the doctrine of metempsychosis, or transmigration of the soul into different bodies. He believed that the universe was created from a shapeless mass of passive matter by the hands of a powerful Being, who was the mover and soul of the world, and of whose substance the souls of mankind were a portion. The time and place of death of this great philosopher are unknown, but some suppose that he died at Metapontum about 497 B. C.

Py'thon. A celebrated serpent sprung from the mud and stagnated waters which remained on the surface of the earth after the deluge of Deucalion. Apollo killed the monster.

Q

Quadra'tus. A surname given to Mercury, because some of his statues were four-sided.

Quad'rifron'tis. Janus was sometimes depicted with four faces instead of the usual two, and he was then called Janus Quadrifrontis,

Qui'es. The Roman goddess of rest; she had a temple just outside the Collini gate of Rome.

Quie'tus. One of the names of Pluto.

Quintilia'nus, Mar'cus Fa'bius, a celebrated rhetorician, born in Spain. He opened a school of rhetoric at Rome, and was the first who obtained a salary from the State as a public teacher. He died A. D. 95.

Quin'tus, Cur'tius Ru'fus. A Latin historian supposed to have lived in the reign of Vespasian. He wrote a history of the reign of Alexander the Great. This work is admired for the elegance of its diction.

Quiri'nus. A name given to Mars during war time; and Virgil refers to Jupiter under the same name.

R

Ra'ma. A Hindoo god, who was the terrestial representative of Vishnu.

Rame'ses. A city of Lower Egypt, built as a treasure city by the captive Israelites, under the oppression of Pharoah.

Regil'lus. A small lake in Latium, famous as being the scene of a great Roman victory, which forms the subject of a fine poem by Macaulay, called "The Battle of the

Lake Regillus," included in his "Lays of Ancient Rome."

REG'ULUS, M. ATTIL'IUS. A consul of Rome during the first war with Carthage. He reduced Brundusuim, and in his second consulship he captured a great portion of the Carthaginian fleet. After further successes he was taken prisoner by the Carthaginians. He was sent from Carthage to Rome to solicit peace, on his promise to return if their proposals were declined. He advised the Romans not to make peace, and returned to Carthage where he was tortured to death.

RHADAMAN'THUS. A son of Jupiter (Zeus) and Europa. He reigned in the Cyclades, where his rule was characterized by marked justice and impartiality.

ROM'ULUS. According to tradition the founder of Rome. He was a son of Mars and Ilia, and was twin brother of Remus. The twins were thrown into the Tiber, but were saved and suckled by a she-wolf till they were found by Fautulus, a shepherd, who brought them up. Disputes arising between the brothers in reference to the building of the city, Romulus caused Remus to be slain.

ROS'CIUS. A celebrated Roman actor. He died about 60 B. C.

RU'BICON. A small river in Italy. By crossing it, and thus transgressing the boundaries of his province, Cæsar declared war against the senate and Pompey. "Passing the Rubicon" has become a proverbial expression, indicating an irrevocable step taken in any weighty matter.

S

SA'CRA, VI'A. An important street in Rome, where a treaty of peace was made between Romulus and Tatius.

SACRI'FICES were ceremonious offerings made to the gods. To every deity a distinct victim was allotted, and the greatest care was always taken in the selection of them. Anything in any way blemished was considered as an insult to the god. At the time of sacrifice the people were called together by heralds led by a procession of musicians. The priest, clothed in white, was crowned with a wreath made of the leaves of the tree which was sacred to the particular god to whom the sacrifice was offered. The victim had its horns gilt, and was adorned with a chaplet similar to that of the priest, and was decorated with bright-colored ribbons. The priest then said, "Who is here?" to which the spectators replied, "Many good people." "Begone all ye who are profane," said the priest; and he then began a prayer addressed to all the gods. The sacrifice was begun by putting corn, frankincense, flour, salt, cakes, and fruit on the head of the victim. This was called the Immolation. The priest then took a cup of wine, tasted it, and handed it to the bystanders to taste also; some of it was then poured between the horns of the victim, and a few of the saturated hairs were pulled off and put in the fire which was burning on the altar. Then, turning to the east, the priest drew with his knife a crooked line along the back of the beast from the head to the tail, and told the assistants to kill the animal. This was done directly, and the entrails of the victim taken out and carefully examined by the Aruspices to find out what was prognosticated. The carcas was then divided, and the thighs, covered with fat, were put in the fire, and the rest of the animal was cut up, cooked, and eaten. This feast was celebrated with dancing, music and hymns, in praise of the god in whose honor the sacrifice was made. On great occasions as many as a hundred bullocks were offered at one time, and it is said that Pythagoras made this offering when he found out the demonstration of the forty-seventh proposition of the book of Euclid.

SA'GA. The Scandinavian goddess of history.

SAL'AMAN'DERS. The genii who, according to Plato lived in fire.

SAL'AMIS. An island of Attica celebrated for a battle fought there between the fleets of the Greeks and the Persians in which the latter suffered defeat.

SALLUS'TIUS, CRIS'PUS. A celebrated Latin historian. He wrote, among other things, a history of the Catilinian conspiracy, and died thirty-five years before the Christian era.

SAL'II. The priests of Mars who had charge of the sacred shields.

SALMO'NEUS. A king of Elis who, for trying to imitate Jupiter's (Zeus) splendors, was sent by the god straight to the infernal regions.

SARM'OS. One of the principal islands in the Ægaean Sea.

SANCHONI'ATHON. A Phœnician historian born at Berytus, or, as some say, at Tyre. He lived a few years before the Trojan war, and wrote on the antiquities of Phœnicia.

SA'POR. 1. A king of Persia, who succeeded to the throne about the 238th year of the Christian era. He wished to increase his dominions by conquest, but was defeated by Odenatus, who defeated his army with great slaughter. He was assassinated A. D. 273. 2. The second king of Persia by that name. He fought against the Romans, and obtained several victories over them. Died A. D. 380.

SAP'PHO, celebrated for her beauty and poetical talents, was born at Lesbos about 600 B. C. She became enamored with Phaon, a youth of Mitylene, but he not reciprocating her passion, she threw herself into the sea from the rock of Leucadia. Moore alludes to her fatal leap in his "Evenings in Greece":—

> "The very spot where Sappho sung
> Her swan-like music ere she sprung
> (Still holding in that fearful leap,
> By her loved lyre) into the deep,
> And, dying, quenched the fatal fire
> At once, of both her heart and lyre."

SARDANAPA'LUS. The last king of Assyria, celebrated for his luxury and indolence. His effeminacy induced his subjects to conspire against him with success, on which he set fire to his palace and perish in the flames B. C. 820. Byron has made his history the subject of a tragedy, in which he introduces as the heroine, Myrrha, a Greek slave, who sets fire to a pile of inflammable materials which had been raised, and perishes with Sardanapalus, exclaiming as she applies the torch,—

> "Lo!
> I've lit the lamp which lights us to the stars."

SAT'URN. An ancient Latin deity, popularly believed to have made his first appearance in Italy in the reign of Janus, instructing the people in agriculture, gardening, etc., thus elevating them from barbarism to social order and civilization. He was consequently elected to share the government with Janus, and the country was called *Saturnia* after him. His reign came afterwards to be sung by the poets as "the golden age." He was often identified with the Crones of the Greeks. His temple was the State treasury. Ops was his wife. His festivals, *Saturnalia*, corresponded to the Greek *Cronia*. It was customary to offer human victims on his altars till this custom was abolished by Hercules. He is generally represented as an old man bent with age, and holding a scythe in his right had.

Saturn.

SAT'YRI. Demigods whose origin is unknown. They had the feet and legs of a goat, their body bearing the human form. They represent the luxuriant vital powers of nature and are inseparably connected with the worship of Bacchus (Dionysus).

SCÆ'VOLA, MU'TIUS, surnamed Cordus, was famous for his courage. He attempted to assassinate Porsena, but was seized; and to show his fortitude when confronted with Porsena, he thrust his hand into the fire, on which the king pardoned him.

SCIP'IO. The name of a celebrated family at Rome, the most conspicuous of which was Publius Cornelius, afterwards called Africanus. He was the son of Publius Scipio, and commanded an army against the Carthaginians. After obtaining some victories, he encountered Hannibal at the famous battle of Zama, in which he obtained a decisive victory. He died about 184 B. C, in his forty-eighth year.

SCIP'IO, LU'CIUS CORNE'LIUS, surnamed Asiaticus, accompanied his brother Africanus in his expedition in Africa. He was made consul in the year of Rome (A. V. C.) 562, and sent to attack Antiochus, king of Syria, whom he completely routed. He was accused of receiving bribes of Antiochus, and was condemned to pay large fines which reduced him to poverty.

Scip'io, P. Æmilia'nus. Called Africanus the younger. He finished the war with Carthage, the total submission of which occurred B. C. 147. The captive city was set on fire, and Scipio is said to have wept bitterly over the melancholly scene. On his return to Rome he was appointed to conclude the war against Numantia, the fall of which soon occurred, and Scipio had Numantinus added to his name. He was found dead in his bed, and was presumed to have been strangled, B. C. 128.

Scyl'la. A daughter of Nysus, who was changed into a lark for cutting off a charmed lock of her father's hair. She lived in a cave in a great rock between Italy and Sicily; Charybdis was another great rock opposite. The place was very dangerous to navigation.

Sea-horse. A fabulous animal depicted with fore parts like those of a horse, and with hinder parts like those of a fish. The Nereids used sea-horses as riding-steeds, and Neptune (Poseidon) employed them for drawing his chariot. In the sea-horse of heraldry a scalloped fin runs down the back.

Sea-horse.

Seges'ta. A rural divinity who protected corn during harvest time.

Sem'ele. A daughter of Cadmus, and Hermione, the daughter of Mars and Venus (Aphrodite). She was the mother of Bacchus (Dionysus). After death she was made immortal under the name of Thyone.

Semir'amis. A celebrated queen of Assyria, who married the governor of Nineveh, and at his death she became the wife of King Ninus. She caused many improvements to be effected in her kingdom, as well as distinguishing herself as a warrior. She is supposed to have lived 1965 years before the Christian era.

SELEN'CUS. The name of several kings of Syria.

SEN'ECA, M. ANNÆ'US, the Latin rhetorician, lived at Rome during the reign of Augustus and Tiberius.

SEN'ECA, L. ANNÆ'US, at an early period of his life, was distinguished by his talents. He became preceptor to Nero, in which capacity he gained general approbation. The tyrant, however, determined to put him to death, and he chose to have his veins opened in a hot bath, but death not ensuing, he swallowed poison, and was eventually suffocated by the soldiers who were in attendance. This occurred in his fifty-third year, and in the sixty-fifth of the Christian era. His works, which were numerous, were chiefly on moral subjects.

SERA'PIS. One of the Egyptian deities, supposed to be the same as Osiris. He had a magnificent temple at Memphis, another at Alexandria, and a third at Canopus.

SESOS'TRIS. A celebrated king of Egypt, who lived long prior to the Trojan war. He was ambitious of military fame, and achieved many conquests. On his return from his victories he employed himself in encouraging the fine arts. He destroyed himself after a reign of forty-four years.

SIBYL. A name common to certain women mentioned by Greek and Roman writers, and said to be endowed with a prophetic spirit. Their number is variously stated, but is generally given as ten. Of these the most celebrated was the Cumæan sibyl (from Cumæa in Italy), who appeared before Tarquin the Proud, offering him nine books for sale. He refused to buy them, whereupon she went away, burned three, and returned offering the remaining six at the original price. On being again refused she destroyed other three, and offered the remaining three at the price she asked for the nine. Tarquin, astonished at this con-

Sibyl of Delphi.

duct, bought the books, which were found to contain directions as to the worship of the gods and the policy of the Romans. These books, or books professing to have this history, were kept with great care at Rome, and consulted from time to time by oracle-keepers under the direction of the senate. They were destroyed at the burning of the temple of Jupiter. Fresh collections were made, which were finally destroyed by the Christian emperor Honorius. The Sibylline Oracles referred to by the Christian Fathers belong to early ecclesiastical literature, and are a curious mixture of Jewish and Christian material, with probably here and there a snatch from the older pagan source.

SEVE'RUS, LU'CIUS SEPTIM'IUS. A Roman emperor, born in Africa, noticeable from his ambition. He invaded Britain and built a wall in the north as a check to the incursions of the Caledonians. He died in York in the 211th year of the Christian era.

SILE'NUS. A demigod, who is represented generally as a fat old man riding on an ass, with flowers crowning his head.

SIL'IUS ITAL'ICUS, C. A Latin poet who retired from the bar to consecrate his time to study. He imitated Virgil, but with little success. His poetry, however, is commended for its purity. He died about A. D. 25.

SIMON'IDES. A celebrated poet of Cos who lived B. C. 538. He wrote elegies, epigrams, and dramatic pieces, esteemed for their beauty.

SIRE'NES. The Sirens. They lured to desruction those who listened to their songs. When Ulysses sailed past their island he stopped the ears of his companions with wax, and had himself tied to the mast of his ship. Thus he passed with safety, and the Sirens, disappointed of their prey, drowned themselves. In works of art they are often represented as having partly the form of birds, sometimes only the feet of a bird.

Siren.

> Next where the Sirens dwell ye plough the seas!
> Their song is death, and makes destruction please.
> POPE.

SIS'YPHUS. Son of Æolus aud Enaretta. After death he was condemned, in the infernal regions, to roll a stone to the summit of a hill, which always rolled back, and rendered his punishment eternal.

SLEIP'NER. The eight-legged horse of Odin the chief of the Scandinavian gods.

SMYR'NA, one of the most ancient and flourishing cities of Asia Minor, and the only one of the great cities on its western coast that has survived to this day.

SOC'RATES. The most celebrated philosopher of antiquity, born near Athens, whose virtues rendered his name venerated. His independence of spirit created for him many enemies, and he was accused of making innovations in the religion of the Greeks. He was condemed to death by drinking hemlock, and expired a few moments after imbibing the poison, in his seventieth year, B. C. 400. His wife was Xanthippe, remarkable for her shrewish disposition, for which her name has become poverbial. Plato was his disciple.

SOL. The sun. The worship of the god Sol is the oldest on record, and though he is sometimes referred to as being the same as the god Apollo, there is no doubt he was worshipped by the Egyptians, Persians, and other nations long before the Apollo of the Greeks was heard of.

SO'LON, one of the wise men of Greece, was born at Salamis and educated at Athens. After traveling over Greece he returned, and was elected archon and sovereign legislator, in which capacity he effected numerous reforms in the State, binding the Athenians by a solemn oath to observe the laws he enacted for one hundred years. After this he visited Egypt, and on returning to Athens after ten years' absence, he found most of his regulations disregarded by his countrymen. On this he retired to Cyprus, where he died in his eightieth year, 558 B. C.

SOM'NUS, son of Nox and Erebus, was one of the infernal deities, and presided over sleep.

SOPH'OCLES. A celebrated tragic poet of Athens. He was

distinguished also as a statesman, and exercised the office of archon with credit and honor. He wrote for the stage, and obtained the poetical prize on twenty different occasions. He was the rival of Euripides for public applause, each having his admirers. He died at the age of ninety-one, 406 B. C. Only seven of his tragedies are extant; the most famous are "Œdipus Tyrannus," "Antigone," and "Electra."

SOPHONIS'BA. A daughter of Hasdrubal, the Carthaginian, celebrated for her beauty. She married Syphax, prince of Numidia, and when he was conquered by the Romans she became a captive to their ally, the Numidian general Masinissa, whom she married. This displeased the Romans and Scipio ordered Masinissa to separate from Sophonisba, and she, urged to this by Masinissa, took poison, about 203 B. C.

SOZ'OME. A historian who died 450 A. D. He wrote an important work on ecclesiastical history.

SPAR'TA, also called Lacedaemon, the capital of Lacoma and the chief city of Peloponnesus of Greece. It disputed with Athens the supremacy of the whole of Greece and the Peloponnesia war (431 B. C.) ended in the overthrow of the Athenian power. They, however, were in turn overthrown by the Thebans at Leuctra B. C. 371. No other single State ever gained the supremacy in Greeee that Sparta possessed until Greece was conquered by Philip of Macedon.

SPHINX. A monster, having the head and breasts of a woman, the body of a dog, the tail of a serpent, the wings of a bird and paws of a lion. The Sphinx was sent into the neighborhood of Thebes by Juno, where she propounded enigmas, devouring those who were unable to solve them. One of the riddles proposed was: What animal walked on four legs in the morning, two at noon, and three in the evening? Œdipus solved it, giving as the meaning, man who, when an infant, crawled on his hands and feet, walking erect in

Greek Sphinx, from a sculpture in British Museum

manhood, and in the evening of life supporting himself with a stick. On hearing the solution the Sphinx destroyed herself. The Egyptian Sphinx was a figure of somewhat similar shape, having the body of a lion (seldom winged), and a human (male or female) or animal head. The human-headed figures have been called androsphinxes; those with the head of a ram criosphinxes, and those with the head of a hawk hieracosphinxes. The Egyptian Sphinx was probably a purely symbolical figure, having no historical connection with the Greek fable, and the Greeks may have applied the term sphinx to the Egyptian statues merely on account of an accidental external resemblance between them and their own figures of the sphinx.

Egyptian Sphinx, from the Louvre Museum, Paris.

STAGI'RA. A town on the borders of Macedonia, where Aristotle was born; hence he is called the Stagirite.

STA'TIUS, P. PAPIN'IUS. A poet, born at Naples in the reign of Domitian. He was the author of two epic poems, the Thebais in twelve books, and the Achilleis in two books.

STA'TOR. A Roman surname of Jupiter, describing him as staying the Romans in their flight from an enemy.

STEN'TOR. One of the Greeks who went to the Trojan war. He was noted for the loudness of his voice, and from him the term "stentorian" has become proverbial.

STERTIN'IUS. A stoic philosopher, whom Horace calls in derision the eighth of the wise men.

STESICH'ORUS, of Sicily, a celebrated Greek poet, contemporary with Sappho, is said to have been born B. C. 632. His poems are mainly lyric, and only a few fragments remain.

STO'IC. A celebrated sect of philosophers founded by Zeno. They preferred virtue to all other things, and regarded everything opposed to it as an evil.

Stra'bo. A celebrated geographer, born at Amasia, on the borders of Cappadocia. He flourished in the age of Augustus. His work on geography consists of seventeen books, and is admired for its purity of diction.

Styx. A celebrated river of the infernal regions. The gods held it in such veneration that they always swore by it, the oath being inviolable.

Sueto'nius, C. Tranquil'lus. A Latin historian who became secretary of Adrian. His best known work is his Lives of the Cæsars.

Sue'vi. One of the greatest and most powerful races of ancient Germany. They occupied the larger portion of all Germany.

Sul'la. See Sylla.

Sulpic'uis, P. Rufus, one of the most distinguished orators of his time, born B. C. 124. In the great civil war he attached himself and fortunes to the cause of Marius.

Syb'aris. A town on the bay of Tarentum. Its inhabitants were distinguished by their love of ease and pleasure, hence the term "Sybarite."

Syl'la (or Sulla), L. Corne'lius. A celebrated Roman, of a noble family, who rendered himself conspicuous in military affairs, and became antagonistic to Marius. In the zenith of his power he was guilty of the greatest cruelty. His character is that or an ambitious, tyrannical and resolute commander. He died about seventy years B. C., aged sixty.

Sylves'ter. The name of Mars when he was invoked to protect cultivated land from the ravages of war.

Sy'phax. A king of the Masæsyllii in Numidia, who married Sophonisba, the daughter of Hasdrubal. He joined the Carthagenians against the Romans, and was taken by Scipio as a prisoner to Rome, where he died in prison.

Syra'cuse. The wealthiest and largest town in the island of Sicily. It was founded B. C. 734 by the Greeks.

Syr'ia. A country of western Asia, lying along the eastern end of the Mediterranean Sea, between Asia Minor and Egypt. Syria included the districts of Phœnice and Palestine. The principal city of Syria was Damascus.

Syrinx. The name of the nymph who, to escape from the

importunities of Pan, was by Diana changed into reeds, out of which he made his celebrated pipes, and named them "The Syrinx."

T

Tac'ita. The goddess of Silence.

Tac'itus, C. Corne'lius. A celebrated Latin historian, born in the reign of Nero. Of all his works the "Annals" is the most extensive and complete. Other of his works are in "History of the Grammar" and "Life of Agricola," his father-in-law. His style is marked by force, precision, and dignity, and his Latin is remarkable for being pure and classical. He probably died about 117 A. D.

Taci'tus, M. Clau'dius. A Roman, elected emperor by the Senate when he was seventy years of age. He displayed military vigor, and as a ruler was a pattern of economy and moderation. He died in the 276 year of the Christian era.

Ta'gus. One of the principal rivers of Spain.

Tan'talus. A king of Lydia, father of Niobe and Pelops. He is represented by the poets as being, in the infernal regions, placed in a pool of water which flowed from him whenever he attempted to drink, thus causing him to suffer perpetual thirst; hence the origin of the term "tantalising." Speaking of this god, Homer's Ulysses says: "I saw the severe punishment of Tantalus. In a lake, whose waters approached to his lips, he stood burning with thirst, without the power to drink. Whenever he inclined his head to the stream, some deity commanded it to be dry, and the dark earth appeared at his feet. Around him lofty trees spread their fruits to view; the pear, the pomegranate, and the apple, the green olive, and the luscious fig quivered before him, which, whenever he extended his hand to seize them, were snatched by the winds into clouds and obscurity."

Taren'tum. An important city founded by the Greeks on the western coast of Italy.

Tan'is. A very ancient city or lower Egypt.

Tarquin'ius Pris'cus. The fifth king of Rome, was son of

Demaratus, a native of Greece. He exhibited military talents in the victories he gained over the Sabines. During peace he devoted attention to the improvement of the capital. He was assassinated in his eightieth year, 578 years B. C.

TARQUIN'IUS SUPER'BUS. He ascended the throne of Rome after Servius Tuilius, whom he murdered, and married his daughter Tullia. His reign was characterized by tyranny, and eventually he was expelled from Rome, B. C. 510; surviving his disgrace for fourteen years, and dying in his ninetieth year. He was the last of the kings of Rome.

TARPEI'A. Daughter of S. Tarpeius, the governor of the Roman citadel on the Saturnian Hill, afterward called the Capitoline, was tempted by the gold on the Sabine bracelets to open a gate of the fortress to the Sabines. As they entered, they threw their shields upon her and crushed her to death. Her name was preserved by being given to the "Tarpeian rock," a part of the Capitoline Hill.

TAR'SUS. The chief city of Cilicia, at the foot of Mount Taurus. It was of unknown antiquity, some asscibing its foundation to the Assyrian king, Sardanapalus. It became a Roman province B. C. 66, through the successful campaign of Pompey in the East.

TAR'TARUS. One of the regions of hell, where, accordiug to Virgil, the souls of those who were exceptionally depraved were punished.

TAUR'I. A wild and savage people in Sarmatia, who sacrificed all stangers to a goddess whom the Greeks liked to Artemis.

TELEG'ONUS. Son of Ulysses and Circe. After Ulysses had returned to Ithaca, Telegonus was sent by Circe in search of his father. He was cast on the shore of Ithaca by a storm, and, being hungry, plundered the fields. Ulysses hearing this, went forth against the stranger and was slain by him. Telegonus carried the body of Ulysses to Circe in Aræa. He afterwards married Penelope.

TELEM'ACHUS. Son of Penelope and Ulysses. At the end of the Trojan war he went in search of nis father, whom, with the aid of Minerva, he found. Aided by Ulysses he delivered his mother from the suitors that beset her.

TEM'PE. A valley in Thessaly through which the river Peneus flows into the Ægaean. It is described by the poets as one of the most delightful places in the world.

TECMES'SA, the daughter of the Phrygian king Teleutas, whose territory was raided by the Greeks during the Trojan war. She was taken prisoner by Ajax by whom she had a son Eurysaces.

TEREN'TIA, wife of Cicero, the orator. She was a woman of sound sense and great resolution. She was divorced from Cicero B. C. 46, and Jerome states that she was married to Sallust the historian. She lived to be 103 years old.

TEREN'TIUS, PUB'LIUS (TERENCE). A native of Africa, celebrated for the comedies he wrote. He was twenty-five years old when his first play was produced on the Roman stage. Terence is admired for the purity of his language and the elegance of his diction. He is supposed to have been drowned in a storm about 159 B. C.

TERMI'NUS. The Roman deity that presided over boundaries or landmarks. He was represented with a human head, without feet or arms, to intimate that he never moved wherever he was placed.

TERPSICH'ORE. One of the Muses, daughter of Jupiter and Mnemosyne. The inventress and patroness of the art of dancing and lyrical poetry. She is generally represented with a lyre, having seven strings, or a plectrum in the hand, sometimes in the act of dancing, and crowed with flowers.

Terminal Statue of Pan, British Museum.

Terpsichore—Antique Statue in the Vatican.

TER'EUS. Was a son of Mars. He married Procne, daughter of the king of Athens, but became enamored of her sister Philomela, who, however, resented his attentions, which so enraged him that he cut out her tongue. When Procne heard of her husband's unfaithfulness she took a terrible revenge (see Itys). Procne was turned into a swallow, Philomela into a nightingale, Itys into a pheasant, and Tereus into a hoopoo, a kind of vulture—some say an owl.

TEREN'TIA'NUS MAURUS, a Roman poet who flourished about 100, A. D.

TERTULLIA'NUS, J. SEPTIM'IUS FLOR'ENS. A celebrated Christian writer of Carthage who lived A. D. 196. He was originally a pagan, but embraced Christianity, of which faith he became an able advocate.

TEU'CER, son of the river-god Scamander by the nymph Idæa, was the first king of Troy, whence the Trojans are sometimes called *Teucri*.

TERPAN'DER. The father of Greek music, and through it, of lyric poetry. He was born in the island of Lesbos, and flourished about 700 B. C. He added three new strings to the lyre, which previously had only four.

THA'IS. A celebrated women of Athens, who accompanied Alexander the Great in his Asiatic conquests. She is alluded to by Dryden in his famous ode, "Alexander's Feast:"—

> "The lovely Thais by his side
> Sate like a blooming Eastern bride
> In flower of youth and beauty's pride."

THALI'A. One of the Muses. She presided over festivals and comic poetry; the Muse of comedy and the patroness of pastoral and comic poetry. She is generally represented with a comic mask, a shepherd's staff, or a wreath of ivy.

THAN'YRIS. A skillful singer, who presumed to challenge the Muses to sing, upon condition that if he did not sing best they might inflict any penalty they pleased. He was, of course, defeated, and the Muses made him blind.

Thalia, Antique statue in the Vatican.

THEMIS'TOCLES. A celebrated general born at Athens. When Xerxes invaded Greece, Themistocles was entrusted with the care of the fleet, and at the famous battle of Salamis, fought

B. C. 480, the Greeks, instigated to fight by Themistocles, obtained a complete victory over the fomidable navy of Xerxes. He died in the sixty-fifth year of his age, having, as some writers affirm, poisoned himself by drinking bull's blood.

THA'LES. One of the seven wise men of Greece, born at Miletus in Iona. His discoveries in astronomy were great, and he was the first who calculated with acuracy a solar eclipse. He died about 548 years B. C.

TEUTON'I, a powerful people of Germany who invaded Gaul and the Roman diminion about 100 B. C. The name Teutones is not a collective name for the whole people of Germany, but only of a particular tribe who dwelt near the Baltic sea.

THE'BÆ. Was the capital of Thebais or upper Egypt. It was reputed to be the oldest city in the world. It was at the height of its splendor as the capital of Egypt, and as a chief seat of the worship of Ammon, about B. C. 1600. The fame of its greatness had reached Homer, who describes it as having a hundred gates. Its glory fell when the Persian invasion under Cambyses took place.

THEOC'RITUS. A Greek poet who lived at Syracuse in Sicily 282, B. C. He distinguished himself by his compositions, of which some are extant, among them about thirty Idyls and some Greek epigrams.

THEODO'SIUS, FLA'VIUS. A Roman emperor surnamed Magnus from the greatness of his exploits. The first years of his reign were marked by conquests over the Barbarians. In his private character Theodosius was an example of temperance. He died in his sixtieth year, A. D. 395, after a reign of sixteen years.

THEODO'SIUS SECOND became emperor of the Western Roman empire at an early age. His territories were invaded by the Persians, but on his appearance at the head of a large force they fled, losing a great number of their army in the Euphrates. Theodosius was a warm advocate of the Christian religion. He died, aged forty-nine, A. D. 450.

TRE'BÆ. The chief city in Bœotia, in Greece. No city is more celebrated in the mythical ages of Greece than

Thebes. The Trebans obtained the supremacy of Greece by defeating the Spartans at the battle of Leuctra, B. C. 371. Their glory was short-lived, for Alexander destroyed the city B. C. 336.

THEOPHRAS'TUS. A native of Lesbos. Diogenes enumerates the titles of more than 200 treatises which he wrote. He died in his 107th year, B. C. 288.

THE'MIS. Daughter of Cœlus (Uranus) and Terra, was married to Jupiter (Zeus), by whom she became the mother of the Horæ, Astræa, and Mœræ. In the Homeric poems Themis is the personification of the order of things established by law, custom, and equity, whence she is described as reigning in the assemblies of men, and by the command of Jupiter, convening the gods. She lived in Olympus, and is said to have been in possession of the Delphic oracle before Apollo.

THERMOP'YLÆ. A narrow pass leading from Thessaly into Locris and Phocis, celebrated for a battle fought there, B. C. 480, between Xerxes and the Greeks, in which three hundred Spartans, commanded by Leonidas, resisted for three successive days an enormous Persian army. Byron, in an apostrophe to Greece, thus refers to the famous conflict:—

"Who now shall lead thy scatter'd children forth,
And long accustom'd bondage uncreate?
Not such thy sons who whilome did await,
The hopeless warriors of a willing doom,
In bleak Thermopylæ's sepulchral strait.
Oh! who that gallant spirit shall resume,
Leap from Eurotas' banks, and call thee from the tomb!"

THERSI'TES. A deformed Greek, in the Trojan war, who indulged in ridicule against Ulysses and others. Achilles killed him because he laughed at his grief for the death of Penthesilea. Shakspeare, who introduces Thersites in his play of "Troilus and Cessida," describes him as "a deformed and scurrilous Grecian."

THE'SEUS, king of Athens and son of Ægeus by Æthra, was one of the most celebrated heroes of antiquity. He caught the bull of Marathon and sacrificed it to Minerva (Athena). After this he went to Crete among the seven youths sent yearly by the Athenians to be devoured by the Minotaur, and by the aid of Ariadne he slew the monster. He ascended his father's throne B. C. 1235. Pirithous, king of Lapithæ, invaded his territories, but the two became firm friends. They descended into the infernal regions to carry off Proserpine, but their intentions were frustrated by Pluto. After remaining for some time in the infernal regions, Theseus returned to his kingdom to find the throne filled by an usurper, whom he vainly tried to eject. He retired to Scyros, where he was killed by a fall from a precipice.

Thes'pis. A Greek poet of Attica, supposed to be the inventor of tragedy, B. C. 536. He went from place to place upon a cart, on which he gave performances. Hence the term "Thespians," as applied to wandering actors. He is called the father of Greek tragedy.

Thersa'lie, the largest division of Greece.

The'on. The name of two mathematicians who are often confounded. The first is of Smyrna, best known as an arithmetician, who lived in the time of Hadrian. The second is Theon the younger, of Alexandria, the father of Hypatia.

Ther'icles. A potter of Corinth, whose works became very celebrated throughout Greece. Some hold that he was a contemporary of Aristophanes, but others deny the existence of Thericles altogether, and contend that the name of the vases ascribed to him is a descriptive one derived from the figures of animals (Theria), with which they were adorned.

Thessalon'ica. An ancient city in Macedonia. It was visited by the Apostle Paul about A. D. 53, and about two years afterwards he addressed two epistles to his converts in that city.

The'tis. A sea deity, daughter of Nereus and Doris. She married Peleus, their son being Achilles, whom she plunged into the Styx, thus rendering him invulnerable in every part of his body except the heel by which she held him.

This'be. A beautiful girl of Babylon, beloved by Pyramus.

THRAC'IA. A large country north of Macedonia, to which it was added by Philip.

THRASYBU'LUS. A famous general of Athens, who, with the help of a few associates, expelled the Thirty Tyrants, B. C. 401. He was sent with a powerful fleet to recover the Athenian power on the coast of Asia, and after gaining many advantages, was killed by the people of Aspendus.

THOR. The Scandinavian war god (son of Odin), who had rule over the ærial regions, and, like Jupiter, hurled thunder against his foes.

THOR'S BELT. Is a girdle which doubles his strength whenever the war god puts it on.

THRA'SEA, P. PÆTUS. A distinguished Roman senator and stoic philosopher in the reign of Nero. He appears to have made the younger Cato his model, of whose life he wrote an account. He incurred the hatred of Nero, and was condemned to death A. D. 66.

THOTH. An Egyptian divinity whom the Greeks considered to be identical with Hermes (Mercury). He was regarded as the inventor of the sciences and arts, and especially of speech and hieroglyphics or letters. He is represented as a human figure with the head of a lamb or ibis.

THUCID'YDES. A celebrated Greek historian born at Athens. He wrote a history of the events connected with the Peloponnesian war. He died at Athens in his eightieth year, B. C. 391.

Thoth, from a bronze in the British Museum.

THUL'E. An island in the northern part of the German ocean, regarded by the ancients as the most northerly point on the whole globe. It is supposed that the island is what is known as Iceland.

TIBE'RIUS, CLAUDIUS NE'RO. The second Roman emperor, 14-37 A. D. In his early years he entertained the people with magnificent shows and gladiatorial exhibitions, which made him popular. At a later period of his life he retired to the island of Capreæ, where he indulged in vice and debauchery. He died aged seventy-eight, after a reign of twenty-two years.

Tibul'lus, Au'lus Al'bius. A Roman knight celebrated for his poetical compositions. His favorite occupation was writing love poems. Four books of elegies are all that remains of his compositions. He died B. C. 18.

Ti'bur. One of the most ancient towns of Latium, sixteen miles northeast of Rome. Under the empire it was a favorite country place for wealthy Romans who built magnificent villas there.

Tigran'es. A king of Armenia, who reigned B. C. 96–56. He assumed the title of king of kings. His power was greatly strengthened by an alliance with Mithridates the Great, king of Pontus. He was defeated by the Romans under Lucullus, in 68 B. C., and thoroughly conquered by Pompey 66 B. C.

Timo'leon. A celebrated Corinthian, son of Timodemus and Demariste. When the Syracusians, oppressed with the tyranny of Dionysius the Younger, solicited aid from the Corinthians, Timoleon sailed for Syracuse with a small fleet. He was successful in the expedition, and Dionysius gave himself up as a prisoner. Timoleon died at Syracuse, amid universal regret.

Ti'mon. A native of Athens, called the Misanthrope from his aversion to mankind. He is the hero of Shakspeare's play of "Timon of Athens," in which his churlish character is powerfully delineated.

Timo'theus. A famous musician in the time of Alexander the Great. Dryden names him in his well-known ode, "Alexander's Feast:"

"Timotheus, placed on high
Amid the tuneful choir,
With flying fingers touched the lyre;
The trembling notes ascend the sky,
And heavenly joys inspire."

Tire'sias. A celebrated prophet of Thebes. Juno deprived him of sight, and, to recompense him for the loss, Jupiter bestowed on him the gift of prophecy.

Tiro, M. Tullius. The freedman of Cicero, to whom he was an object of tender affection. He was the amanuensis of the orator, and was himself a writer of no little repute. It is supposed that Tiro was the chief person to whom we owe the preservation of Cicero's letters and works.

TISIPH'ONE. One of the Furies, daughter of Nox and Acheron.

TISSAPHER'NES. A famous Persian who governed lower Asia in B. C. 414. He aided Artaxerxes against Cyrus and greatly harrassed the ten thousand Greeks in their famous retreat.

TITA'NES. The Titans. A name given to the gigantic sons of Cœlus and Terra. The most conspicuous of them are Saturn, Hyperion, Oceanus, Iapetus, Cottus, and Briareus.

TITHO'NUS. The husband of Aurora. At the request of his wife the gods granted him immortality, but she forgot at the same time to ask that he should be granted perpetual youth. The consequence was that Tithonus grew old and discrepit, while Aurora remained as fresh as the morning. The gods, however, changed him into a grasshopper, which is supposed to moult as it gets old, and grows young again.

TIT'YUS. A son of Jupiter (Zeus). A giant who was thrown into the innermost hell for insulting Diana (Artemis). He, like Prometheus, has a vulture constantly feeding on his ever-growing liver.

TI'TUS VESPASIA'NUS. Roman emperor, 79–81 A. D. Son of Vespasian and Flavia Domitilla, known by his valor, particularly at the siege of Jerusalem. He had been distinguished for profligacy, but on assuming the purple, he became a model of virtue. His death, which occasioned great lamentations, occurred A. D. 81, in the forty-first year of his age.

TRAJA'NUS, M. UL'PIUS CRINI'TUS. A Roman emperor, 98–117 A. D. His services to the empire recommended him to the notice of the emperor Nerva, who adopted him as his son, and invested him with the purple. The actions of Trojan were those of a benevolent prince. He died in Cilicia, in August, A. D. 117, in his sixty-fourth year, and his ashes were taken to Rome and deposited under a stately column which he had erected.

Tribu'ni Ple'bis. Magistrates at Rome created in the year B. C. 261. The office of Tribune to the people was one of the first steps which led to more honorable employments.

Tri'mur'ti. The name of the later Hindoo triad or trinity, Brahma, Vishnu, and Siva, conceived as an inseperable unity. The sectaries of Brahma, Vishnu and Siva respectively make their god the original deity from which the trinity emanates; but considered separately Brahma is the creating, Vishnu the preserving, and Siva the destroying principle of the deity, while Trimurti is the philosophical or theological unity which combines the three separate forms in one self-existent being. The Trimurti is represented symbolically as one body with three heads, Vishnu at the right, Siva at the left, and Brahma in the middle.

Trimurti, from Coleman's Hindoo Mythology.

Triptol'emus. Son of Oceanus and Terra, or, according to some authorities, son of Celeus, king of Attica, and Neæra. He was in his youth cured of a severe illness by Ceres (Demeter), with whom he became a great favorite. She taught him agriculture, and gave him her chariot drawn by dragons, in which he traveled over the earth, distributing corn to the inhabitants.

Tri'ton. A sea deity, son of Neptune (Poseidon) and Amphitrite. He was very powerful, and could calm the sea and abate storms at his pleasure. He dwelt with his father and mother in a golden palace on the bottom of the sea. The later poets speak of Tritons in the plural as a race of subordinate sea deities. Their appearance is differently described, though they are always conceived as presenting the human figure in the upper part of their bodies, while the lower part is that of a fish. A common characteristic of Tritons in poetry as well as in art is a shell-trumpet which they blow to soothe the restless waves of the sea.

Triton—from antique mosaic.

MYTHOLOGICAL DICTIONARY.

TRIUM'VIRI. Three magistrates appointed to govern the Roman state with absolute power.

TRO'JA or Troy (Ilium), was the famous city the contest for which forms the subject for Homer's Iliad. Its exact location has always been in dispute, some even doubting the existance of such a place. It is supposed to have been situated on a moderate elevation at the foot of Mount Ida, in the northwest part of Mysia, and nearly surrounded by the river Scamander. The mythical account ascribes the founding of the kingdom to Teucer, whose grandson was Tros, who was the father of Ilus, who called the city Ilium after himself and Troja for his father. The next king was Laomedon, and after him Priam. In the reign of Priam the city was taken by the confederated Greeks after a ten years' seige (.See Helene, Priamus, Achilles, Ajax, Hector, Ulysses, Agamemnon.) The date of the capture of Troy is usually set at B. C. 1184.

TULLI'A. The daughter of Cicero.

TUL'LIUS SERVIUS. The sixth king of Rome.

TUL'LUS HOSTIL'IUS succeeded Numa as king of Rome. He was of a warlike disposition, and distinguished himself by his expedition against the people of Alba, whom he conquered.

TUS'CULUM. An ancient town of Latium, and one of the most strongly fortified places in Italy, both by nature and art.

TYPHŒ'US or TY'PHON. A famous giant, son of Tartarus and Terra, who had a hundred heads. He made war against the gods, and was put to flight by the thunderbolts of Jupiter, who crushed him under Mount Ætna.

" . . Typhon huge, ending in snaky twine."
MILTON.

TY'PHON. In Egyptian mythology the god who tried to undo all the good work effected by Osiris.

TYRTÆ'US. A Greek elegiac poet, born in Attica. Of his compositions none are extant except a few fragments.

U

UL'LER. The Scandinavian god who presided over archery and duels.

UL'TOR. "The avenger," a surname of Mars, the god of war.

ULYS'SES (ODYSSEUS). A famous king of Ithaca, son of Anticlea and Laertes, or, according to some, of Sisyphus. He married Penelope, daughter of Icarius, on which his father resigned to him the crown. He went to the Trojan war, where he was esteemed for his sagacity. On the conclusion of the war he embarked for Greece, but was exposed to numerous misfortunes on his journey. In his wanderings, he, with some of his companions, was seized by the Cyclops Polyphemus, from whom he made his escape. Afterwards he was thrown on the island of Æea, where he was exposed to the wiles of the enchantress Circe. Eventually he was restored to his own country, after an absence of twenty years. The adventures of Ulysses on his return from the Trojan war form the subject of Homer's Odyssey.

UNX'IA. A name of Juno, relating to her protection of newly-married people.

UT ICA. The greatest city of ancient Africa after Carthage, was a Phœnician colony. It took sides in the last Punic war with Rome against Carthage, and was rewarded with the greater part of the latter's dominion.

URA'NIA. One of the Muses, daughter of Jupiter (Zeus) and Mnemosyne. She presided over astronomy. She is generally represented holding in her left hand a celestial globe to which she points with a little staff.

UT'GORD LO'KI. In Scandinavian mythology the king of the giants.

V

VALENTINIA'NUS. The first emperor of Rome, 364-375 A. D., son of Gratian, raised to the throne by his merit and valor. He obtained victories over the Barbarians in Gaul and in Africa, and punished the Quadi with severity. He broke a blood-vessel and died, A. D. 375. Immediately after his death his son

Urania, antique statue in the Vatican.

Valentinian the Second, was proclaimed emperor. He was robbed of his throne by Maximus, but regained it by the aid of Theodosius, emperor of the East. He was strangled by one of his officers. He was remarkable for benevolence and clemency. The third Valentinian was made emperor in his youth, and on coming to maturer age he disgraced himself by violence and oppression. He was murdered A. D. 454.

VALERIA'NUS, PUB'LIUS LICIN'IUS. A celebrated Roman emperor, 253-260, A. D, who on ascending the throne, lost the virtues he had previously possessed. He made his son Gallienus his colleague in the empire. He made war against the Goths and Scythians. He was defeated in battle and made prisoner by Tabor, king of Persia, who put him to death by torture.

VAL'HAL'LA. The Scandinavian temple of immortality, inhabited by souls of heroes slain in battle.

VA'LI. The Scandinavian god of archery.

VALLO'NIA. The goddess of valleys.

VAR'IUS RUFUS. One of the most distinguished poets of the Augustan age; the companion and friend of Virgil and Horace. By the latter he is placed in the first rank of epic bards. Only a few fragments of his poems are extant.

VAR'RO. A Latin author, celebrated for his great learning. He wrote no less than five hundred volumes, but all his works are lost except a treatise "De Re Rustica," and another "De Lingua Latina." He died B.C. 28, in his eighty-eighth year.

VARU'NA. In Hindoo mythology a deity represented in the Vedic hymns as of great and manifold powers—the guardian of immorality, cherisher of truth, and seizer and punisher of ill-doers, the forgiver of sins, protector of the good, and the exerciser generally of unlimited control over man. Latterly he became the god of waters, the cause of rain, lord of rivers

Varuna, the god of Waters.

and the sea, the Hindoo Neptune (Poseidon) indeed. He is represented as a white man, four armed, riding on a sea animal, generally with a noose in one of his hands and a club in another, with which he seizes and punishes the wicked.

VENT'I. The winds. Borean (north wind), Eurus (east wind), Notus (south wind), and Tephyrus (west wind).

VE'NUS (Aphrodite). One of the most celebrated deities of the ancients; the goddess of beauty, and mother of love. She sprang from the foam of the sea, and was carried to heaven, where all the gods admired her beauty. Jupiter (Zeus) gave her in marriage to Vulcan (Hephæstus), but she intrigued with some of the gods, and, notably, with Mars, their offspring being Hermione, Cupid, and Anteros. She became enamored of Adonis, which caused her to abandon Olympus. Her contest for the golden apple, which she gained against her opponents Juno (Ceres) and Minerva (Athena), is a prominent episode in mythology. She had numerous names applied to her, conspicuous among 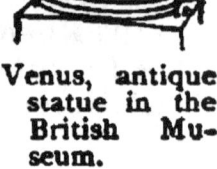 Venus, antique statue in the British Museum. which may be named Anadyomene, under which cognomen she is distinguished by the picture, representing her as rising from the ocean, by Apelles. She was known under the Grecian name of Aphrodite Venus indirectly caused the Trojan war, for, when the goddess of discord had thrown among the goddesses the golden apple inscribed "To the fairest," Paris adjudged the apple to Venus, and she inspired him with love for Helen, wife of Menelaus, king of Sparta. Paris carried off Helen to Troy, and the Greeks pursued and besieged the city (see Helen, Paris, and Troy). Venus is mentioned by the classic poets under the names of Aphrodite, Cypria Urania, Astarte, Paphia, Cythera, and the laughter loving goddess. Her favorite residence was at Cyprus. Incense alone was usually offered on her altars, but if there was a victim it was a white goat. Her attendants were Cupids and the Graces. She is represented as the highest ideal of female beauty and love, and was naturally a favorite subject with the ancient poets and artists, some of her statues being among the noblest remains of Greek and Roman sculpture. Among the most famous of her statues are the Venus of Cnidus, by Praxiteles, of which the Venus de Medici, found in the Villa Hadriana at Tivoli, is supposed to be a free copy, and the Venus of Milo or Melos, found in the island of Melos. Among the modern statues one of the most famous is the Venus of Canova, where she is represented as issuing from the bath.

VERCINGET'ORIX. A celebrated chief of the Gauls, who carried on the war with great ability against Julius Cæsar, B. C. 52.

VERRES C. A celebrated Roman prætor of Sicily, where he acquired immense wealth by his extortionate cruelty. The inhabitants brought him to trial and engaged Cicero to accuse him. Verres was condemned and banished from Rome.

VERTI'COR'DIA. A Roman name of Venus, signifying the power of love to change the hard-hearted. The corresponding Greek name was Epistrophia.

VES'TA. A goddess, daughter of Rhea and Saturn. One of the great divinities of the ancient Romans, identical with the Greek *Hestia*, the virgin goddess of the heart. She was worshipped along with the Penates at every meal, when the family assembled around the hearth, which was in the center of the room. Æneas was said to have brought the sacred fire, which was her symbol, from Troy, and brought it to Rome, where it was preserved in her temple which stood on the Forum. To prevent this fire from becoming extinguished it was given into the superintendence of six stainless virgins, called *vestals*. The Palladium, a celebrated statue of Pallas, was sup-

Vesta—Antique statue, Florence.

posed to be preserved within her sanctuary, where a fire was kept continually burning.

VERTUM'NUS. God of spring, or, as some mythologists say, of the seasons; the husband of Pomona, the goddess of orchards.

VESPASIA'NUS, TI'TUS FLA'VIUS. A Roman emperor 77-79 A. D., of obscure descent. He began the siege of Jerusalem, which was continued by his son Titus. He died A. D. 79, in his seventieth year.

VESTA'LES. The Vestals, priestesses consecrated to the service of Vesta. They were required to be of good families and free from blemish and deformity. One of their chief duties was to see that the sacred fire of Vesta was not extinguished.

VIRGIL'IUS, PUB'LIUS MA'RO, Called the prince of the Latin poets, was born at Andes, near Mantau, about 70 years B. C. He went to Rome, where he formed an acquaintance with Mæcenas, and recommended himself to Augustus. His Bucolics were written in about three years, and subsequently he commenced the Georgics. His Æneid, the great Latin Epic poem, is supposed to have been undertaken at the request of Augustus. Virgil died in his fifty-first year, B. C. 19.

VIRGIN'IA. Daughter of the centurion, L. Virginius. She was slain by her father to save her from the violence of the decemvir, Appius Claudius.

VISH'NU. In Hindoo mythology the god who, with the other two great gods, Brahma and Siva, forms the *trimurti*, or trinity; the Preserver, considered by his worshippers to be the supreme god of the Hindoo pantheon. In the early Vedas he appears as the manifestation of the sun, and was regarded as the most exalted deity, this rank being accorded to him by the later writers of the Ramayana, the Mahabharata, and more especially of the Puranas. The Brahmanic myths relating to Vishnu are characterized by the idea that, whenever a great physical or moral disorder affected the world, Vishnu descended in a small

Vishnu on his Man-bird Garuda.

portion of his essence to set it right. Such descents are called *avataras* or *avatars*, and consist in Vishnu's assuming the form of some wonderful animal or superhuman being, or as being born in human form of human parents, and always endowed with miraculous power. Vishnu is sometimes represented as riding on Garuda, a being half bird and half man, as holding in one of his four hands a conch-shell blown in battle, in another a disc, an emblem of supreme power; in the third a mace as the emblem of punishment, and in the fourth a lotus as a type of creative power.

VIRGIN'IUS. A valiant Roman; father of Virginia. (See Virginia.) The story of Virginius and his ill-fated daughter is the subject of a well known tragedy, "Virginius," one of the early productions of J. Sheridan Knowles.

VITEL'LIUS, Roman emperor from January to December, A. D. 69. He was succeeded by Vespasian.

VOLUP'TAS, the personificator of sensual pleasure, was honored with a temple in Rome.

VULCA'NUS. The god who presided over fire, and who was the patron of those who worked in iron. According to Homer, he was the son of Jupiter and Juno, and was so deformed that, at his birth, his mother threw him into the sea, where he remained nine years; but other writers differ from this opinion. He married Venus at the instigation of Jupiter. He is known by the name of Mulciber. The Cyclops were his attendants, and with them he forged the thunderbolts of Jupiter. The Roman poets transferred all the stories which are related of the Greek Hephæstus to their own Vulcan, the two divinities becoming in the course of time completely identified. By some writers he is said to have been born lame, but by others his lameness is attributed to his having been thrown from Olympus. Vulcan patronized handicraftsmen of every kind, and to this or to his lameness the poets most frequently refer. In sculpture he is

Vulcan, from an antique.

generally represented as a strong, bearded man, with a hammar and pincers and a pointed cap.

VULCA′NIA were Roman festivals in honor of Bacchus, at which the victims were thrown into the fire and burned to death.

W

WO′DEN. The Anglo-Saxon form of the Scandinavian god Odin; Wednesday is called after him.

X

XANTHIP′PE or XANTIP′PE. The wife of Socrates, remarkable for her ill-humor and fretful disposition. She was a constant torment to her husband, and on one occasion, after bitterly reviling him, she emptied a vessel of dirty water on him, on which the philosopher coolly remarked: "After thunder, rain generally falls."

XAN′THUS. A lyric poet who lived about B. C. 650.

XENOC′RATES. An ancient philosopher born at Caledonia, and educated in the school of Plato, whose friendship he gained. Died B. C. 314.

XEN′OPHON. A celebrated Athenian, son of Gryllus, famous as a general, philosopher, and historian. He joined Cyrus the Younger in an expedition against Artaxerxes, king of Persia, and after the decisive battle of Cunaxa, in which Cyrus was defeated and killed, the skill and bravery of Xenophon became conspicuous. He had to direct an army of ten thousand Greeks, who were now more than six hundred leagues from home, and in a country surrounded by an active enemy. He rose superior to all difficulties till the celebrated "Retreat of the Ten Thousand" was effected; the Greeks returning home after a march of two hundred and fifteen days. Xenophon employed his pen in describing the expedition of Cyrus, in his work the "Anabasis." He also wrote the "Cyropædia," "Memorabilia," "Hellenica," etc. He died at Corinth in his ninetieth year, about 360 B. C.

XER′XES. Succeeded his father Darius on the throne of Persia (B. C. 485-465). He entered Greece with an immense army, which was checked at Thermopylæ by the valor of three hundred Spartans under King Leonidas, who, for three successive days successfully opposed the enormous forces of Xerxes, and were at last slaughtered. From this period the fortunes of Xerxes waned. His fleet being defeated at Salamis, and mortified with ill-success, he hastened to Persia, where he gave himself up to debauchery, and was murdered in the twenty-first year of his reign, about 464 years B. C

Y

YAMA. In Hindoo mythology the god of departed spirits and the appointed judge and punisher of the dead; the embodiment of power without pity, and stern, unbending fate. He is generally represented as crowned and seated on a buffalo, which he guides by the horns. He is four-armed and of austere countenance. In one hand he holds a mace, in another a noose which is used to draw out the bodies of men, the souls which are doomed to appear before his judgment seat. His garments are of the color of fire, his skin is of a bluish green.

Yama.

Y'MIR. The Scandinavian god, corresponding to Chaos of the Greeks.

Z

ZA'MA. A town of Numidia, celebrated as the scene of the victory of Scipio over Hannibal, B. C. 202.

ZE'NO. A celebrated philosopher, the founder of the sect of Stoics, was born at Citium in Cyprus. He opened a school in Athens, and soon became noticed by the great and learned. His life was devoted to sobriety and moderation. He died at the age of ninety-eight, B. C. 264.

ZE'NO. A philosopher of Elea or Velia, in Italy. He was the disciple, or, according to some, the adopted son of

Parmenides. Being tortured to cause him to reveal his confederates in a plot he had engaged in, he bit off his tongue that he might not betray his friends.

Zeno'bia. A celebrated princess of Palmyra, the wife of Odenatus. After her husband's death (A. D. 266), the Roman emperor, Aurelian, declared war against her. She took the field with seven hundred thousand men, and though at first successful, she was eventually conquered. Aurelian, when she became his prisoner, treated her with great humanity and consideration. She was admired for her literary talents as well as her military abilities.

Zeph'yr. The god of flowers, a son of Æolus and Aurora, the west wind. See Favonius.

Zeus. See Jupiter.

Zeux'is. A celebrated painter born at Heraclea. He flourished 468 B. C. He painted some grapes so naturally, that the birds came to peck them on the canvas; but he was disgusted with the picture, because the man painted as carrying the grapes was not natural enough to frighten the birds.

Zo'ilus. A sophist and grammarian of Amphipolis, B. C. 259. He became known by his severe criticisms on the works of Isocrates and Homer.

Zoroas'ter. A king of Boctria, supposed to have lived in the age of Ninus, king of Assyria, some time before the Trojan war. He rendered himself known by his deep researches in philosophy. He admitted no visible object of devotion except fire, which he considered the proper emblem of a Supreme Being. He was respected by his subjects and contemporaries for his abilities as a monarch, a lawgiver, and a philosopher, and, though many of his doctrines may be deemed puerile, he had many disciples. The religion of the Parsees of the present day was founded by Zoroaster.

Zos'imus. A Greek historian, who lived about the year 410 A. D. He wrote a history of some of the Roman emperors, which is characterized by graceful diction, but he indulges in malevolent and vituperative attacks on the Christians in his history of Constantine.

APPENDIX A.

The Equivalent Names of Various Personages of Ancient Mythology Among the Greeks and Romans.

GREEK.	ROMAN.
Aphrodite,	Venus.
Apollo,	Apollo.
Ares,	Mars.
Artemis,	Diana.
Athena,	Minerva.
Cronos,	Saturn.
Demeter,	Ceres.
Dike,	Justitia.
Dionysus,	Bacchus.
Ge,	Terra.
Hades,	Pluto.
Helios,	Sol,
Hephæstus,	Vulcan.
Hera,	Juno.
Hermes,	Mercurius.
Hestia,	Vesta.
Leto,	Latona.
Persiphone,	Proserpina.
Poseidon,	Neptune.
Uranus,	Coelus.
Zeus,	Jupiter.

Appendix B.

A Short Chronological Table of Some of the Most Important Facts in Roman History.

B. C.
- 753 Foundation of Rome, Romulus, first king.
- 716 Numa Pompilius, second king.
- 673 Tullus Hostilius, third king.
- 640 Ancus Martius, fourth king.
- 616 Tarquin, the elder, fifth king.
- 578 Servius Tullius, sixth king.
- 543 Tarquin, the Proud, seventh king.
- 510 Expulsion of Tarquins and establishment of the Republic.
- 509 War with Etruscans.
- 493 War with Volscians.
- 489 Volscians, under Coriolanus, sack Rome.
- 483 War with Veii.
- 461 Struggles between patricians and plebians.
- 458 War with Sabines—Cincinnatus, dictator.
- 452 Appointment of the Decemvirs.
- 451 Laws of the Twelve Tables promulgated. Death of Virginia—Decemvirs deposed.
- 390 Rome taken by the Gauls.

389 Rome rebuilt.
343 First Samnite War.
340 Latin War—Latins become subject to Rome.
326 Second Samnite War.
321 Surrender of Romans to Samnites at Caudine Forks—War continued.
304 End of Samnite War.
298 Third Samnite War.
281 Pyrrhus arrives in Italy to help Tarentines.
280 Romans defeated by Pyrrhus.
275 Defeat of Pyrrhus.
264 First Punic War.
241 End of first Punic War.
239 Ennius born.
234 Birth of Cato.
225 War with the Gauls.
224 Plautus flourished.
218 Second Punic War.
212 Hannibal takes Tarentum.
208 Hannibal gains victory of Venusia.
202 Hannibal defeated by Scipio at battle of Zama.
191 War with Antiochus.
149 Third Punic War.
146 Destruction of Carthage.
133 Murder of T. Gracchus.
121 Death of C. Gracchus.
111 Jurgurthine War.
106 Birth of Cicero.
90 Social War.
86 Death of Marius.
78 Death of Sulla.

70 Birth of Virgil.
69 War with Mithradates.
65 Birth of Horace.
63 Death of Mithradates.
63 Cicero Consul.
59 Birth of Livy.
58 Julius Cæsar's first campaign in Gaul.
49 Civil war between Cæsar and Pompey.
48 Death of Pompey.
44 Death of Julius Cæsar.
43 Second Triumvirate formed by Octavianus (afterward the Emperor Augustus), Antony and Lepidus.
Birth of Ovid.
31 Battle of Actium—Antony defeated.
27 Octavianus receives title of Augustus. Beginning of Empire.
19 Death of Virgil.
18 Horace flourished.
8 Death of Horace.

A. D.
1 Birth of Jesus Christ.
14 Death of Augustus.

APPENDIX C.

A Short Chronological Table of Some of the Most Important Facts in the History of Ancient Greece.

C.
- 750 Miletus, the greatest city of Greece.
- 734 Syracuse founded.
- 693 Glaucus flourished.
- 687 The Empire of the Medes begun.
- 657 Byzantium founded by the Megarians.
- 647 Pisander flourished.
- 625 Arion flourished.
- 611 Sappho flourished.
- 594 Solon, ruler of Athens.
- 586 The Seven Wise Men flourished.
- 572 Æsop flourished.
- 559 Cyrus begins to reign in Persia. Anacreon flourished.
- 538 Babylon taken by Cyrus.
- 529 Death of Cyrus.
- 525 Birth of Æschylus.
- 518 Birth of Pindar.
- 514 Hipparchus slain.
- 510 Expulsion of Hippias from Athens.

The Ten Tribes instituted at Athens.
500 Birth of Anaxagoras.
499 Ionian revolt.
495 Birth of Sophocles.
492 Persians invade Europe and add Macedonia to the Persian Empire.
489 Miltiades died.
485 Xerxes, King of Persia, succeeding Darius.
484 Herodotus born.
483 Ostracism of Aristides.
481 Themistocles leading man in Athens.
480 Xerxes invades Greece and takes Athens.
479 Persians expelled from Greece.
477 Commencement of Athenian supremacy.
471 Thucydides born.
469 Pericles flourished.
468 Socrates born.
465 Death of Xerxes.
464 Zeno flourished.
461 Pericles leading man in Athens.
449 Renewal of war with Persia.
439 Athens at the height of its glory.
431 Beginning of great Peloponnesian war, which lasted twenty-eight years.
430 Plague rages at Athens.
429 Plato born.
427 Aristophanes flourished.
425 Eruption of Mt. Ætna.
421 Truce for fifty years between Athenians and Lacedæmonians.
406 Death of Euripides and Sophocles.

404	Government of Athens in the hands of the "Thirty Tyrants."
401	Retreat of the ten thousand Greeks.
399	Death of Socrates.
367	Aristotle comes to Athens.
359	Accession of Philip, King of Macedonia.
356	Birth of Alexander the Great.
352	Demosthenes flourished.
336	Death of Philip and accession of Alexander the Great.
334	Alexander commences war against Persia.
323	Death of Alexander at Babylon. Division of his Empire among his generals.
280	Rise of Achæan League.
147	Macedonia becomes a Roman province.
146	Destruction of Corinth. Greece becomes a Roman province.